LAST OF THE REDMEN

A MEMOIR BY

BILLY MITARITONNA

Thank you for reading my memoir. Please go to my website www.lastoftheredmen.com for more information on how to become a part of the "Walk-on" community.

Feel free to view pictures and articles about *Last of the Redmen* and please leave comments about my story.

Once again, thank you for reading!

- Billy Mitaritonna

LAST OF THE REDMEN

A MEMOIR OF A
ST. JOHN'S BASKETBALL WALK-ON

SOMETIMES YOU ONLY NEED ONE PERSON
TO BELIEVE YOU CAN SUCCEED

By Billy Mitaritonna

I would like to dedicate my memoir to the following people:

My wife, Kristen

Thank you for always believing in me in my professional or personal goals. You are an amazing wife, mother, and my best friend. I know you always have my back and that's why it was important to have your approval to write my memoir. I will always love and respect you!

My parents

Although you are both looking down on us now, I find myself thinking about both of you everyday and the lessons you taught me. You were great role models and I try to be the best father and husband possible. I miss you and I hope you are proud of our family and the life we have built.

My children

Jackie, Courtney, and Brendan- you're the reason why I work so hard to provide for our family and I love you very much. The sky's the limit for each of you to succeed. Please know how proud I am of each of you!

Coach Jim Graffam

Outside of my parents, you are the most important person in becoming the man I am today. Thank you for taking a chance on me when no one else would. You cannot understand how much you mean to me in my personal and professional life. Henry Adams said, "A teacher affects eternity; he can never tell where his influence stops" This quote says it all about your influence on all of your players.

CHAPTER ONE

PROLOGUE: WHY WRITE THIS STORY?

IT WAS a frigid Friday night in December of 2007, and my Half Hollow Hills High School West Colts varsity basketball team had just defeated our crosstown rival, Hills East. This was the second win in a streak that lasted twenty-three games, and resulted in the very first Suffolk County Championship in the history of Hills West basketball. And this was the first time my father Angelo watched us that season, too. He'd just flown in from his winter home in Las Vegas for the holidays. As we sat at a restaurant with one of our oldest friends from Rosedale, Walter Johnson, Angelo gave nothing but praise to our team and the way I coached. My father always had kind words, as well as constructive criticism, after a game. He had a way of telling you how to look at a situation in a different way, so that it would sound non-threatening. His basketball and coaching knowledge was vast, and I knew it carried weight. He liked how our team moved the ball on offense. Angelo also liked how I got my bench significant playing time in a blowout win, though he felt it was most important that we'd raised money for the American Cancer Society in our annual Coaches vs. Cancer game. Always coaching, always being a good father to his son.

But it was something he said to me on Christmas Eve weeks later, as I sat across from him after dinner, that stuck with me. My arm was in a sling, having had arthroscopic shoulder surgery that morning, and I was resting on a couch in the living room in front of our fireplace. My three young children ran around the house as my wife cleaned up after dinner. Angelo was always my biggest supporter, and on this night, he expressed his emotions openly. This was a rarity. Angelo was a quiet, reserved, and positive influence on everyone he met. His mantra was "Actions, not words." On that night, maybe it was the Maker's Mark talking, but he said something very special to me. It was my father who taught me the important aspects in life, and sports had always been the center of our relationship.

He said with a serious look on his face, "You should write a book."

I replied, with a smile on my face, "Dad, are you kidding me? You can't be serious."

"Your story of playing basketball in college to coaching high school hoops at Hills West is amazing and inspirational. I know I haven't told you this as much as I should have, but I am so proud of you."

As he got up to go to bed, he hugged me, and I helped him up the stairs due to his fifty-year-old knee injury. I waited for him to go to bed before I started crying. I don't know if he'd ever said anything that profound to me up until that point, though I was thirty-five years old, with a beautiful family and a successful career. When he said that, all the pain in my shoulder went away. He had a special way of making me feel like the best son on earth.

So at the end of our Suffolk County Championship 2007-08 season, I decided to start to write my story to honor my dad. Angelo was an amazing role model, teacher, mentor, and father. He did so much for me over the years—how could I not grant his wish? I hope my relationship with my father and sports can inspire others: parents, coaches, teachers, and mentors, on and off the playing field. My father is the one who has inspired me my entire life.

As a coach, I realize the impact I can have on a young person or a team. Outside of my mother and father, no one has been more important to my development as a person and a teacher than Jim Graffam. He was my basketball coach at Westbrook College in Portland, Maine, from 1990-92. This man took me out of obscurity from a schoolyard in Queens and made my dream of playing college basketball a reality. Coach Graffam has been a mentor and friend for over twenty-eight years. He is the most important person in my life, outside of my family. Sometimes you only need one person in your life to believe in you to achieve greatness. I was fortunate to have two strong basketball influences.

At home, I have been blessed with four people who love me unconditionally. My wife Kristen is the perfect companion. There is nothing you cannot get through in life if you have a True Companion. (Credit to the artist Marc Cohn; that's our wedding song.) She has put up with me since 1995 and raised our three children while I spent countless hours teaching and coaching. She has always encouraged me to pursue my professional goals by taking the family burden onto her shoulders. This is not an easy thing to do with young children, but Kristen manages to get it done. She is a rare combination of positive energy and love. My three wonderful children, Jackie, Courtney, and Brendan, have given me years of laughter, love, and pride. They are the reason I work so hard to be the man I have become.

Finally, I am a social studies teacher and basketball coach, not a writer. However, I love to tell a good story, and I use that in the classroom and on the basketball court. My students and players have always enjoyed my past experiences and learned from them. Please enjoy my story.

CHAPTER TWO

FAMILY FIRST

LET me start by saying how proud I am of my parents. Angelo Mitaritonna married Mary Patricia Gibbons in August of 1971, in the Yorkville section of the Upper East Side of Manhattan. They'd met three years earlier in a bar called T.T.'s, in the same neighborhood. At the time of their marriage, Angelo owned a luncheonette in Brooklyn, and Mary was an emergency room nurse at St. Clare's Hospital in Hell's Kitchen.

Both traveled the world in the 1960s. Dad played basketball at Erasmus High School in Brooklyn with a great player named Johnny Lee and NBA legend Doug Moe. He was recruited to play for the University of Utah in the 1950s and played against basketball royalty Bill Russell and Casey Jones at San Francisco in the 1956 NCAA tourney. My father said he'd never seen a person dominate a basketball game defensively like Bill Russell. After a year and a half at Utah, he transferred to a small Division 2 school in Hattiesburg, Mississippi called William Carey College, where he played for two more years. They called him "the Golden Greek" due to his jet-black hair, even though he was 100% Italian. My dad could really shoot the basketball. He claimed to have the first "one-handed jump shot" in Brooklyn when everyone else shot with two hands. After college, his good friend John Sullivan recruited him to play for the Washington Generals, as he entertained thousands of people while losing to the Harlem Globetrotters. Angelo played against Meadowlark Lemon and even Wilt Chamberlain for one tour. Wilt left Kansas University early after his junior year in college to join the Globetrotters until he was drafted in 1960 by the Philadelphia Warriors. My father loved Wilt; he always said, "Wilt was the best guy to hang out with on the road." Red Klotz was my father's coach and treated my father like his own son. They were friends for life. Angelo played for three years, but his dream of playing pro ball died with his knee injury.

My mom heard a speech as a Georgetown nursing student in January of 1961 in which an Irish-Catholic President named John F. Kennedy stated, "Ask not what your country can do for you, but what you can do for your country." She was so moved by his words that she left Georgetown Nursing and was part of the first group of female nurses to join the Peace Corps. My mom was sent to Tanganyika in Africa for two years. At the same time, thousands of miles apart, both Mom and Dad were making lasting contributions to our global community. Both performed a valuable service for children. My dad made kids smile in every game he played. As a Washington General, he was a part of the show, and loved watching the kids enjoy the Globetrotters from Honolulu to Havana. Mom worked with the children of Tanganyika to help make their lives easier and healthier.

Finally, both were in their mid-30s and ready to settle down. They were married in 1971, moved to Rosedale, Queens, and had me in 1972. As my father said with a smile on his face, "You showed up too early and I had to give up my N.I.T. championship tickets at Madison Square Garden," when Mom went into labor on March 23. My father wanted to name me Vito, after Don Corleone from *The Godfather*. (It premiered on March 24th, the day I was born). Mom said absolutely not. She won that battle, and I was named after my father's Uncle Billy, who died in World War II—but also Bill Bradley, from the New York Knicks. My mom agreed, because both people were outstanding Americans. Mom and Dad wanted the best of everything for our family, and Bill Bradley was the perfect mix of academics and athletics.

We lived in a second-floor apartment on 147th Drive off Brookville Boulevard in Rosedale, Queens. My childhood was as happy as it could be in the late 1970s. Taking walks to Brookville Park with my parents, picnics at Beach 20th street in Far Rockaway, or just having a catch in the apartment with Dad when Mom wasn't looking. In 1975, my sister Joanne was born, and our family was complete. We were located twenty minutes away from my Italian grandparents, Isabelle and Nick Mitaritonna, who lived with my Aunt Barbara and Uncle Lou in Howard Beach, Queens. Forty-five minutes away lived my Irish grandparents, Marie and Martin Gibbons, who lived in Manhattan. We would visit them often, and it was always fun because they could really cook.

In the late 1970s, we faced a lot of adversity. My mom had open heart surgery in 1976. I don't really remember it, but a lot of my relatives would come over and watch us. My father's luncheonette in Flatbush, Brooklyn was burned to the ground during the blackout of 1977. Hours after the blackout hit, my father got a call from a police officer who would come to his store frequently. The police officer watched the flames coming from his building. There was nothing my father could do. New York City was on fire, and my dad had to sit there and take it. He lost everything he had put into his business after many years. It set us back, and he needed to find a job with flexible hours so he could bring my mom to various doctors when she needed to go. My father took a job as a NYC taxi driver and worked seven days a week for twenty years straight. I think about his work ethic often; it was selfless and amazing.

In 1979, my mother went back to work and acquired hepatitis on the job at St. Clare's Hospital. As a result, she had to stay home for almost a year to recover. I remember this year because as a second-grader at St. Pius X School in Rosedale, I was taken care of by a wonderful community. My second-grade teacher, Sister Angela, looked after me in school, and my friends' parents did the same. These were rough times for our family, but as my mom felt better, we started looking for a house to buy in Rosedale so I could stay at St. Pius X with my friends.

CHAPTER THREE

ROSEDALE, QUEENS

WHAT A PLACE TO GROW UP, and what an education I received from this neighborhood. As Chazz Palminteri wrote in his story *A Bronx Tale*, "I got two educations, one at school and one in the streets." He was right on the money. Located in the most southeast section of Queens, Rosedale was made up of middle-class families, mostly Irish, Italian, German, and African-American. My parents told me of racial problems that existed in Rosedale when I was younger. (In fact, Rosedale was the focus of a 1976 Bill Moyers documentary called *Rosedale: The Way It Is*, which captured the growing racial divide within our town.) As I got older, I saw it firsthand in the schoolyards and in the streets. My sister and I attended St. Pius X Catholic School for two reasons:

1. My parents were devout Catholics.
2. St. Pius X encouraged diversity. The local public schools were mostly all white, and my parents wanted us to be open-minded regarding skin color and race.

Don't get me wrong, Rosedale was a great place to grow up, but looking back now, I really must thank my parents for making the decision to send me to Catholic school instead of public school in Rosedale. The education was outstanding, everyone was treated equally, and the teachers and nuns were tough on all of us. I saw the difference between my classmates and the students who went to public school. We learned at an early age that people are people, no matter what skin color. I was lucky to have parents who were tolerant of others and believed in the teachings of the Catholic Church.

In first grade, I became best friends with Quincy Roberts, who lived two blocks away toward the park on Brookville Blvd. I would go to Quincy's house after school when my mom was sick. His parents and grandmother were very good to me. Frequently, we would walk to Dwayne Richards' house, who lived two blocks away in the other direction. The three of us would walk to the bus stop together every morning. After school, we would go to each other's houses and play with our Star Wars toys, or play tag. Tom and Kevin McLaughlin, who lived around the corner on 148th Avenue, were older but looked out for us. During the summer of 1979, we had a mini-baseball league in the McLaughlins' driveway. My mom thought it was awesome that we played baseball around the corner, as long as Quincy walked with me. I learned the rules of baseball and how to hit live pitching. Tom and Kevin gave out paper plate awards around the time of the death of Thurman Munson, the great Yankee catcher. The summer before, my father had convinced me to be a Mets fan, and I was forbidden to like the Yankees, but we felt bad for the Munson family because Thurman was only 32 years old at the time of his death. All baseball fans rallied around the Yankees, and Tom and Kevin taught me everything they knew about America's pastime. This was the year I fell in love with baseball and the team with the worst record: the New York Mets.

CHAPTER FOUR

THE BEST COACH I'VE EVER HAD

IN THE 1979-1980 SCHOOL YEAR, Dad signed me up for Rosedale soccer and Little League baseball. I was good at both sports, but I lived for baseball, especially the Mets.

Let me backtrack for a moment. My dad had told me I could root for anyone except the Yankees, because I was not allowed to like "the evil empire." Dad was a true-blue Brooklyn Dodger fan, so I had to choose another team. I liked the color blue, I lived in Queens, and Angelo always said to "root for the underdog." My love for the Mets started in 1978 and is still going strong today. Every time we would drive home from my grandmother's apartment in Manhattan, he would take the Triboro Bridge and drive on the Grand Central Parkway by Shea Stadium at night, so I could look at the lights coming from the ballpark. I absolutely loved going there with my father. It was our special place, and he knew I loved being at Shea Stadium with him.

Playing in the instructional league in the spring of 1980 for Rosedale baseball was great, but not fun. Hitting off a tee was lame. I learned how to hit live pitching from Dad and the McLaughlins when I was seven. Playing in the street around the corner with older kids made me a better player. At age eight, I was so good that Rosedale Little League moved me up to play with the nine-year-olds in the farm league. Dad was always working or taking care of Mom, so he didn't have time to see me play a lot, but promised to coach me next year.

As the spring of 1981 rolled around, my dad kept his word and became the head coach of the minor division White Sox. There were ten teams in each division at the time, as baseball was king in Rosedale. We played our games at Brookville Park, and my father was able to move me up a league, so I was one of the only nine-year-olds playing with ten and eleven-year-olds.

My dad drafted my good friend Nuffy from St. Pius. He was the biggest, toughest kid in the neighborhood. Nuffy was built like a man in the 5th grade. He had broad shoulders and muscles everywhere, with a mean streak to match. No one messed with Nuffy in Rosedale. His grandmother and my mother sat together in church, so Nuffy always looked after me like a little brother. Dad thought the world of him, and drafted other kids he knew from St. Pius as well. This made me more comfortable and more accepted, being the youngest player in the division. We had the players no one else wanted, but our squad ran through the league, winning and having fun in the process. Dad had practices around his work schedule in the gulley at Brookville Park, which was a grass field up against the tennis courts. His philosophy was simple and one I have adopted. Everyone on the team was important, and no one player was bigger than the team. He let anyone try any position and spot in the batting order. It was all about having fun and learning the game. We learned how to bunt, how to hit the cutoff man, how to run the bases more efficiently, and more. My dad always hit me last in the batting order and said I had to pay my dues. However, he did let me play second base (my favorite player was second baseman and Gold Glove winner Doug Flynn from the Mets), but I had to rotate in the field like everyone else. He had a way of keeping everyone happy and fresh. He learned this playing for the legendary Al Bonnie with the Brooklyn Bonnies in the late 1940s.

After each game I played, my father would say these two very important sentences to me in the car. "Hey, Bill, I really enjoyed watching you play today. Did you have fun?" My father was a genuine human being. He played enough sports in his life to realize that you're going to lose more than you win. At an early age, he impressed upon me the importance of having fun with sports. I just wanted to be with him all the time. He always had a way of making me feel like the best son on Earth.

We rolled through the playoffs, and Nuffy's grandmother would buy us pizza after every big game we won. In the championship game, my father did something nice for me and hit me leadoff in the lineup against my St. Pius buddy Pete Trapani. Pete was just as tough as Nuffy, and a good athlete as well. I led off the game with a single to right field, and we didn't stop hitting the entire game. Playing on field four, which was the "good field with the fence," gave us an opportunity to show our stuff, and Nuffy smoked one into the weeds, otherwise known as JFK Airport. After the game, as promised, Nuffy's grandmother bought everyone pizza, and we celebrated like the kids in the Bad News Bears movie. My dad had confidence in me the whole time, but wanted me to work for it. I remember thanking him when we got home, he was so happy for me. But like most early Sunday morning games, he would drive me home and then go to work for eight hours. He had an amazing work ethic that I'm only starting to appreciate now that I have children.

CHAPTER FIVE

GETTING A BACKYARD

AT THE END of the summer of 1981, we finally found a house in Rosedale. No more second-floor apartment, and no more getting yelled at by the landlord for playing too loud. We moved in on Labor Day weekend, and I was so excited to have a backyard, basement, a second-floor bedroom, and a new block of friends to make. On our street were some very nice families. Jeff Wilkins lived in an apartment down at the end of our dead-end block, and he was a year older than me at St. Pius X. I met him over the summer playing baseball, and couldn't believe how tall he was for his age. He was best friends with someone else I had met over the summer (by getting a hit off him), Pete Trapani. Pete lived on the other side of the fence from Jeff, around the corner from our block. It was instant Wiffle Ball games, touch football, and basketball in my backyard. Angelo (from Flatbush, Brooklyn) put up a hoop in the spring of 1982 so we wouldn't have to go to the P.S. 138 schoolyard. He knew what went on in the city schoolyards, but I thought it was great that my friends would come over to play, like Jeff, Pete, Walter Johnson, Timmy O'Leary, Vinnie Cerchione, Ray Sims, and Vinnie Spano.

Vinnie's cousin Mike Spano was on my baseball team over the

summer, and he would come over all the time to play too. Our dead-end block was perfect for holding sporting events, and everyone came to play our crew. There were no three better all-around athletes in Rosedale than Jeff, Pete, and myself. We played every sport: football, basketball, baseball, tennis, soccer, and hockey. I looked up to the both of them like older brothers, and I constantly tried to gain their acceptance by competing every day for their approval. Jeff was so much bigger than myself and Pete that we would take him on, two on one. He was bigger and stronger than us, but I wanted to beat him so badly. When I played him one on one, he kicked my butt every single time. He might have beaten me 1,000 times over a ten-year period. I was able to beat him later in life when I finally caught up to him in height, but as a young man, I was pushed athletically by peer competition.

But more importantly, my parents' hard work paid off, as they were homeowners for the first time. My sister and I had our own rooms, a great basement, and a super backyard. These were all luxuries after ten years of living in a second-floor apartment. I learned to appreciate the little things in life. My parents were excited that we made new friends, lived three blocks from school, and had a new house that we could call our own.

CHAPTER SIX

SCHWINN THRASHER

BASEBALL MEANT the world to me when I was ten, eleven, and twelve. I cried like a baby if my Little League games were rained out. Picture an eleven-year-old kid from Queens crying for a half hour because it rained on a Saturday morning in May. That's how much Little League meant to me. I wanted to compete, and I absolutely loved to prove to everyone how good I was at sports. That's what's missing today, with the over-scheduling of our children. We had a competitive chip on our shoulders. Playing with older kids made me want to prove to them that I could hang. That aspect definitely stayed with me in life. Whenever I ran into a situation where I was over-matched, I rose to the occasion.

I hated September, because baseball was over and it was back to school. In the spring of 1982, when I was ten years old, my dad stayed on to coach me and I finally became an all-star. I loved playing baseball, and Rosedale had some great players. The league was huge, with ten teams in each age group. It also gave me a chance to play against other kids from the neighborhood.

In the spring of 1983, when I was eleven, my father could not afford to miss work anymore, so I was drafted into the majors' division and played for a dedicated baseball coach for the Astros named Richie DeCurtis. Richie was rough around the edges, but knew the game of baseball. He had unique signs in the third base coaching box. If he grabbed his crotch (balls), that meant bunt. If he picked his nose (snot), that meant steal a base. When we won our game, he got us in a huddle and made us yell "assholes" instead of "Astros." These are things that made me laugh when I was a young boy, though they're extremely inappropriate.

Our team was stacked with great athletes, and I played so well that I was selected that spring as the only eleven-year-old on the twelve-year-old Williamsport travel team. I couldn't believe I was the best eleven-year-old baseball player in Rosedale. Richie had a lot to do with that, because he taught the game well. My dream of playing for the Mets one day was looking good, but I was sent mixed messages from my coaches. My role was to learn for the next summer, so it didn't matter how I played. And if I did play, it would be in a blowout. What I didn't understand then is that every game that you play in is important, and that you should play to win. The fun is a product of competing at a high level, and winning is a result of that competition.

As an example of a mixed message, I was put in to pinch hit late in a game and I struck out. I didn't care because next year I would be the man, but my teammates were upset with me. They didn't know what the coaches were telling me, because they wanted to win now. I thought that there was always next year. How wrong I was.

In January of 1984, Jeff and Pete introduced me to the Daily News paper route boss Mr. Havelin so I could get a job delivering the newspaper. You had to be twelve in order to work, but I lied about my age so I could start right away. I was given thirty-five houses on my route, all within five blocks from my home. But I now needed a bike to deliver the paper. My parents laid out $119.00 for my brand-new Schwinn Thrasher. We couldn't afford the very popular Schwinn Mongoose, which cost fifty dollars more. Of course, I would have to pay them back when I made enough money to do so. It was perfect for my route, because I could wrap my delivery bag around the handlebars and whip those papers onto a stoop (not the driveway, like they do today). It was a challenge for me to get the papers out of the house before 7:15 a.m., and I would time myself each day to better myself. My mom was great, because she would rattle her cane against the railing at 6:45 to wake me up. Most days I was already up with my alarm, but I would sprint downstairs, sit on the porch, fold and rubber band the newspaper, and then pack them up. I timed myself by looking at the flashing VCR clock in the living room. This was the fun part. I put on my Walkman, pressed play, and made my run. My record for delivering all thirty-five papers was eight minutes. That's if I hit every stoop with my throws. What a sense of accomplishment each morning, and breakfast was always provided by Mom. She always had a meal waiting.

1984 was a great year for music, but nothing was better than Van Halen. When I put my Walkman on to deliver the Daily News, it was like Eddie Van Halen's guitar was speaking to me. The song "Panama" on the album 1984 was my favorite, so I took a black marker and wrote *Panama* on the silver crossbar. Van Halen's songs just clicked with me, so I bought all of their cassettes and enjoyed their music while delivering the newspaper. My bike was so much fun to ride, no matter what time of year. What a great job for a twelve-year-old boy.

On April Fools' Day of 1984, a week after my twelfth birthday, I did not listen to my father. What a huge mistake I made. My parents and sister were going to the store, but I chose to play roller hockey with the crew on our block. He didn't like me playing hockey, but I did anyway. I never said no to competition, so they left and I stayed home.

It was a beautiful early spring day, as the temperature hit sixty degrees with blue skies above. About an hour after they left, the guys were thirsty, so we took a water hose break. The guys ran into Richie Martinsen's backyard. I sprinted for the hose behind the others and lost my balance on the upgrade of Richie's lawn. My body jerked back to the right, and I landed on my right arm with a thump. To this day, that's the worst pain I have ever felt. My friends thought I was messing around because it was April Fools' Day. I stood up with a scream from a horror movie, and my right wrist was sagging limp. I'd broken both bones in my right wrist. My parents got home and we went to North Shore Hospital. We waited in the emergency room for five hours with people who had bumps, bruises, and bad coughs. As we sat in the ER waiting room, there was one old TV that had the news on in the evening. Marvin Gaye had been shot and killed by his father. Such a sad story—it's amazing what you remember when you're in pain.

The doctor finally x-rayed me and set my arm in a long cast for eight weeks. The official diagnosis was that I'd snapped my ulna and radius bones. June 1st would be the next time I would play a sport again. Missing the first half of the baseball season was worse than the agony of the arm pain. My father was disappointed with me, my coaches were pissed, and I was devastated that I could not play. Adding insult to injury, I picked up the flu in the ER and missed a week of school. There were no MRI tests given, or physical therapy, and so as I found out later in life, I'd torn ligaments in my right wrist, which prevented me from stretching my right hand back ever again.

That one mistake really set me back athletically forever. But there was one positive; this allowed me to work on my left hand for basketball in the backyard. I was never the same in baseball after that injury, although I became an all-star later that season due to my body of work the year before. I played shortstop but couldn't hit my weight. Again our team fell short to our rivals from northern Queens, HBQVB, in the finals, and we did not advance. But I was falling in love with basketball and a team from Queens.

CHAPTER SEVEN

THE BEST BASKETBALL TEAM IN NYC

HEAD COACH LOUIE CARNESECCA, Chris Mullin, Willie Glass, Bill Wennington, Walter Berry, Mark Jackson, Mike Moses, and Shelton Jones: the reason why I fell in love with the game of basketball, the 1984-85 St. John's Redmen.

During the 1984-85 basketball season, I played 7th-grade CYO basketball at St. Joseph's Roman Catholic Church in Hewlett. St. Pius X didn't have a program because there was no gym. My dad was one of the coaches, and we were a below average team. We practiced once a week in Hewlett and played a game on the weekend. I was hooked because I played all the time in my backyard with the guys, and at the St. Pius X schoolyard during recess. There were times when I would wake up extra early in the morning, deliver the Daily News on my paper route, and get to the schoolyard early. There were some great games with Quincy, Dwayne, Jeff, Pete, and anyone else who was there before school. I was starting to love basketball, and baseball became secondary.

St. Pius X would let 7th and 8th-graders go home for lunch if you lived within a certain distance. If it was rainy or too cold, the teachers wouldn't let students go outside for recess, so Jeff, Pete, and myself would go home to eat. My mom would make me the best lunches in a bag, but going home was better: hot soup, sandwiches, and any leftovers from her great cooking the night before. Our games during lunch were legendary, but on Friday, December 7th, I decided to walk home alone at noon. I usually walked home for lunch from school with Jeff and Pete, but these two 8th-graders decided to stay home and go to Green Acres Mall on that rainy day. I left St. Pius X through the cafeteria back doors, as always, and walked across the playground towards the "dirt pile," where new homes were to be built. The rain had stopped, and as I climbed over the small hill onto 253rd Street, a small red car drove past me after I crossed the road. I got to the corner of 253rd and 147th, and two men jumped out of the car and stepped in front of me.

One man, about eighteen years old, asked me in a menacing voice if I had any money. I looked at him and said, "No, I don't."

The other man said, "Come on, white boy, we know you have money. Give it to us now." I put my hands inside my pockets and pulled them inside out to show I wasn't lying.

Now while this was going on, I had what I call that "trust my gut" feeling, and walked quicker around the corner, away from them. The driver of the car pulled around the corner to follow me. At that point, I started to run down the block, in a full sprint, in my ugly brown shoes. The two men chased me on foot, and halfway down the street they caught up to me. They pushed me to the ground and I went into the fetal position. What happened next can best be described as a beatdown. They punched me in the back of the head and the lower back. They kicked me in the thighs and ribs as I screamed for help. When you're in a moment of terror, everything slows down to a crawl. I didn't know how I was going to get out of it, but I heard a voice. It was George from up the block, and he was out to walk his dog. George worked nights, which was why he was outside at noon. I was his newspaper boy. He yelled to me from up the block and asked if I needed help.

George yelled, "Bill, are you okay? Are those your friends?"

I screamed back to him from the ground, "HELP! HELP!"

George responded by sending his Doberman pinscher in my direction. I couldn't see what was going on, but the guy in the car yelled, "Get in the car, hurry! Let's go!"

They stopped hitting me, and I heard the dog barking at the guys while they jumped into the small car. They drove away, and George ran down the block in the middle of the street. He got their license plate number as his dog chased the car down the block. I looked up with anger, fear, and pain, and saw George walking in my direction. He picked me up off the ground and asked if I was okay. Then he drove me home and walked me to my door. This is where I pulled myself together so my mother wouldn't start crying. My Catholic school uniform pants were ripped, and I came home at 12:15, when I usually showed up at 12:05. I walked in the door, and she met me in the living room and asked who George was, the look of fear in her face.

I told her, "Mom, this is George, and he helped me while I was being mugged." She instantly freaked out and started crying as she hugged me to see if I was okay. George introduced himself and told my mom what he'd seen. He was amazing. He left his phone number in case we got the police involved. My mom sat me down on the couch and checked me over like the nurse she was. I had a lot of bumps and bruises, but no blood or breaks. She put me flat on my back on our living room couch and brought in a drink for me. My mom's concern turned to anger pretty quickly, and she called the main office to alert St. Pius X. She spoke to my social studies teacher, Mr. Vallar, and let him know what had gone on as I left school grounds. He said three kids had been thrown out of our school at 11:55, looking for another student. Mr. Vallar told my mom to call the police and make a report. She hung up and asked me if I wanted to call the police. I thought about it for a minute, and my fear turned to anger as well—I said yes. Before she could pick up the phone, another call came in from my social studies teacher from last year, Mr. Russell, to express his concern. These two men were my inspiration to teach social studies. It was nice that they called me at home.

My mother called the police at 12:30, and they showed up twenty minutes later. Two detectives from the 105th precinct knocked on our door, and my mother let them in. I got up off the couch to greet them, and they politely said to sit down and relax. They asked if I needed medical attention, but I wanted to wait until my dad got home. They introduced themselves and asked me exactly what had happened. I explained it and gave them the license plate. They were pleasantly surprised and asked if I wanted to come down to the precinct house to look at mugshots. My mom thought it would be a good idea, so I got in their car with ice on my back and drove to the station. This was going to be an experience for a twelve-year-old boy.

I went into the 105th police station and sat down at the detective's desk. A lot of policemen came up to me and asked if I needed anything—Pepsi, chips, candy—they were very nice. A very young assistant district attorney sat down with me in another room and videotaped my story. They took my deposition and I looked at three full books of mugshots. That was a miserable experience. I finished up, and they had me home by 4:00. My father didn't get home until 5:30 in those days, and my mother was worried about his reaction. He was very mild-mannered and I never really saw him get upset much, so I didn't know why she was concerned.

I spent the next hour and a half relaxing on the couch as the pain in my body started to kick in more and more. My dad walked in at 5:45 and always came in the house with his favorite greeting, "Hey, hey, hey." He looked at me on the couch and instantly knew there was something wrong. Parents have a way of sensing an issue with their children. He asked me what was going on. My mom came in from the kitchen and looked at me. She wanted me to tell him. I looked at my dad and told him what had happened as I ran down the events of the entire day. He asked me if I was okay and if I wanted to see a doctor, and my mom said we were waiting for him to come home first. The detectives recommended to go to Franklin General in Valley Stream when my father got home. Dad tapped me gently on the head, went into his bedroom, and slammed the door. I had never seen that side of him before. Angelo was always calm and cool, but he was incensed after listening to my story. You have to remember, he worked in Manhattan in the 1980s, when crime was rampant and muggings were a daily occurrence. My mom limped into their bedroom and told my father to hang up the phone. He raised his voice for the first time I'd ever heard and told my mom to leave him alone. He yelled, "I know what I'm doing!" My mom told him that the police were coming back later tonight to check on me. She said, "Let the police handle it." They never told me who my dad was going to call, and I never asked.

We went to the hospital for x-rays, and the ER doctor said I was smart to cover up my face, because that's where people bleed the most. I was sent home, and the police detectives were out in front of my house as we pulled up. Again, for the second time in a day, my dad got angry.

Sarcastically, he quipped, "Now you show up to help. Where were you earlier today?" They didn't respond to him as he walked me into the house. He was clearly upset. My mom stepped up and invited the detectives into our home. It was late, and they basically told us that 95% of all muggings go unsolved. They would be in touch if they caught a break in the case, but they weren't optimistic.

We had an unofficial motto with my friends in Rosedale: "If someone makes fun of you, that means they like you." The next day, I received a number of phone calls and visits from my friends, busting my chops. They were relentless. Telling me I was too slow, I had no guts fighting back. I sarcastically thanked Pete and Jeff for not being there to protect me. I was really sore on Saturday, but my mom made me my favorite meal: chicken cutlets, mashed potatoes, and spinach.

But when my dad got home, I could tell he was still upset from the day before. He said, "I know it hurts right now, but you'll be fine down the road. You were in the wrong place at the wrong time, and sometime down the road, the odds will be in your favor and you'll be in the right place at the right time." At twelve years old, that doesn't help much, but he was very right.

On Sunday morning, the telephone rang. It was the detectives from Friday night, and they'd arrested two men matching the description I gave them late Saturday night. They were driving on the other side of Rosedale in a car with the license plates that I'd reported. My mom was amazed and called me downstairs from my bedroom. She put me on the phone with the police. They wanted to bring me in for a lineup to see if I could identify the two people they had in custody. I told them I would call them back. I hung up the phone and sat down with my mom. She explained to me that this would be a good thing that a lot of citizens don't get to experience, and a way to learn about the criminal justice system. I was afraid that they would see me and come get me later on after the trial, when it was over. My dad came home early from work, and he was convinced by my mom to go through the lineup with me. My mom called the 105th precinct, and we were on our way.

When I arrived at the police station, it was different than I'd envisioned. There were teenage kids hanging out in front of the station, just waiting around for something to happen. I thought to myself, *What child would actually hang out at a police station?* We walked in and everyone was so nice to us. The three of us were escorted into the squad room, which was busy. I asked the detectives inside why teenagers were hanging around. First of all, the detective told me, I had very good instincts, and secondly, those kids were waiting around to work lineups. The cops paid them $5 each to stand in a lineup. To me that seemed like a great side job.

We sat down with an assistant district attorney and the two detectives that had taken my report on Friday. The first thing they said to my parents was how courageous it was to come down today, because a lot of citizens were not willing to do so. Also, they mentioned that it was rare that they caught muggers, but George got the license plate, so that was a tremendous help. They put on a video camera to walk me through my statement again. That took a long time. In the back of my mind, I was worried about the lineup. Would these guys be able to see me? If they did, could they find me later? How would I defend myself?

All these questions were answered by the ADA. They explained that the lineup would be easy, and no one would be able to see me. They prepared me for the lineup by showing me another room with no one in it, putting me in the room and trying to look in the mirror to see my parents. That helped a lot. We walked next door into a dark room, where there was a wall with a slot and a handle on it too high for me to view. They brought over a chair for me to stand on. My job was simple. There would be six men in the other room. Pick the number of the man who beat me up. I had to be 100% sure. The detective opened the slot, and I looked through with my parents right behind me. It took me five seconds to see #4 was one of my muggers. No doubt about it. It gave me a freakish feeling to know he was ten feet away from me. They asked me again and reaffirmed my original statement. It was him. The ADA and detectives all gave me a pat on the back and said I did great. They brought in the next six men, and I went through the same process. This time, I wasn't sure, because it was the driver of the car and I didn't get a great look at him. They said it was all right that I didn't get it right, because he'd been arrested on another charge. We went into the squad room and sat with the ADA and detectives, and they asked if I was sure to go through with the charge of assault against this man. I looked at my parents for approval and they nodded. I wanted to get this guy for what he'd done to me, but I was still a little apprehensive. The entire process, from December 7th to the grand jury, the trial, and sentencing took me into eighth grade. I learned a lot about the criminal justice system, but even more about standing up for what's right. Nine months later, he was sentenced to five years probation, and he was not allowed to set foot in Rosedale or he would be immediately arrested and given a year in jail. The ADA said he was going away for a long time on his other charge, and that made us feel better. It was a long ordeal, but one I will never forget. It made me stronger emotionally, and I gained respect for our justice system.

During that winter, a story in college basketball was developing right here in Queens. The St. John's Redmen basketball team was amazing. Head coach Louie Carnesecca was full of emotion and high energy on the sidelines. Smooth-passing Mark Jackson at the point, high-flying forwards Willie Glass and Shelton Jones, big men Walter Berry and Bill Wennington, and the reason why I wanted to play at St. John's: Chris Mullin, who later became an NBA Hall of Famer. I enjoyed watching this team play because they had it all and looked good doing it: great passing, players who could dunk, and Mullin's shooting. My dad said Mullin would sneak into gyms late at night and take 1,000 shots. He would wake up and run six miles in the morning, and then play for three hours during the day during the summer. I wanted to be like Chris. In February of 1985, we didn't have a lot of money, so I took a white t-shirt and wrote the name Mullin on the back in red, complete with the #20. This season was exciting, and the Garden was sold out all the time. I was hooked, as St. John's knocked off Georgetown during the regular season and became #1 in the country. St. John's breezed through the NCAA tourney, and Dad and I watched every game. After defeating Kentucky in the regional semifinal, they beat Jimmy Valvano's NC State Wolfpack on my thirteenth birthday in the regional final. St. John's was heading to the Final Four in Lexington, Kentucky to play Georgetown for the fourth time. I remember being in Vinnie Spano's basement hanging out with him and his cousin Mike. But St. John's didn't have a chance, and Georgetown, led by Patrick Ewing (someone I would have a lot of respect for later on in life) beat the Redmen. I was devastated, and my only pleasure that weekend was watching Villanova knock off Georgetown in the finals two days later in a stunner for the 1985 National Championship.

The 1984-85 basketball season changed my view on sports, and playing for St. John's one day became my dream. Playing baseball for the Mets was no longer important.

CHAPTER EIGHT

CHANGES CONTINUE...

IN THE SPRING OF 1985, baseball started up. When I showed up for the first practice, there were twelve kids from my age group there. I didn't get it, since last year, we'd had ten teams in our league. So what? We would be playing on the big Babe Ruth field, which was regulation size. But that had nothing to do with it. A change was going on in Rosedale, and when you're thirteen years old, you can't really see it.

In the late 1970s, the NYC Board of Education decided to create a tri-community junior high for Rosedale, Laurelton, and Springfield Gardens. Some people in Rosedale didn't want their children getting on a bus and going to Springfield Gardens for junior high school. Most parents would rather send them to the elementary schools that had K-8 classes in Rosedale, but that policy had ended. So these families moved to Long Island when their oldest child finished sixth grade in search of better schools. That left us with just enough players for one team in our age group. Our coaches had a good idea so we could play that summer. They signed us up for the Valley Stream Pony League, which had more than ten teams in it. This is when the issue of race reared its ugly head.

Our team was made up of ten thirteen-year olds from varying backgrounds and races. We had never played together before this season, but we knew each other's abilities. We had kids from St. Pius X, one of which was one of my oldest friends, Dwayne Richards, who was Bahamian. He played third base and I played shortstop. Our head coach was Mr. Farrell, and the assistant coach was my father. Danny Farrell was our center fielder. His father was white and his mother was black, which was rare in the 1980s. He was a good athlete and the funniest kid on the team, which is why he's a comedian in Los Angeles today. We had great pitching and timely hitting. I also felt like I was at the top of my game defensively. I couldn't hit a curveball, and my average was low, but I could stop anything hit in my direction.

We didn't know what we were getting into, but one thing was clear, we were very good. Our team had a record of 20-4 and we won the championship. When it came time to celebrate the Rosedale Angels, the Valley Stream Mail League refused to recognize us and didn't give us trophies because we didn't pay Nassau County taxes. That was their reason. Our coaches told us that trophies are nothing but a waste. If you walk off a field, you know you played your best, and you won, that's all that counts. I never looked at awards or trophies the same way again. All of us inside felt race played a part, and the fact that we had a diverse team made us stronger. I learned one indisputable fact: when you win, people get jealous, and the worst comes out. I don't know if it was racially motivated or not, but we were a team who refused to lose, and got along on and off the field. Our coaches were the difference. Once again, I had fun like in years before, and once again, my father Angelo had a lot to do with it.

CHAPTER NINE

ARCHBISHOP MOLLOY HIGH SCHOOL

IT WAS in the seventh grade that I made the decision to go to Archbishop Molloy High School. There was no other alternative for me. I visited the Catholic high school in Briarwood, Queens, and instantly knew I was going there. Mom fell in love with the school as well; it reminded her of where my uncles had gone for high school in Manhattan.

In the eighth grade, I took the Catholic school entrance exam and got into Archbishop Molloy. Jeff and Pete were already freshmen at Molloy, and I couldn't wait to go. Another choice that people had to make in Rosedale was what public school to go to. Most people moved out, so they didn't have to send their kids to Springfield Gardens. It was an easy decision for my parents, I was going to Catholic school: end of story. I was going to have to travel fifty-five minutes by bus and subway each way to get there, but it was going to be worth it.

Our eighth-grade CYO season at St. Joseph's was our best to date. We had three six-footers in our starting lineup and very good shooting guards. I was a guard who did not have a position. I knew how to play the game, but I couldn't score. Also, I was one of the shortest kids on the team at 5'5". But there were two things I did well: pass and defend. We were pretty successful that season, and the next stop for me was Molloy.

In the fall of 1986 in my freshman year, I experienced a major transition to high school. First of all, Molloy was an all-boys high school, I took tough honors classes, and there were 400 other freshmen who were just as athletic as I was. In late October of 1986, right around the time the Mets were winning the World Series, I went into the freshman basketball tryouts very apprehensive about my chances. I was nervous because I hadn't made many friends, I wasn't one of the bigger players at 5'6", and I didn't want to let my father down. In addition to that, Jeff had made the freshman team the year before and started. He was one of the best players in his sophomore class. I thought it would be cool because Jeff and I could practice together, travel to games, and get on the bus on Sunday mornings to go to Molloy with our awesome basketball gear on.

Tryouts came, and it seemed like 200 out of the 400 freshmen tried out. I made it through the first two cuts very optimistically, but on the last day, I was let go. My name was not on the list. I was devastated to not make the team, but I wasn't upset because I got cut—I was upset because I wanted to make it for Dad. He had done everything for me to get me ready, and I'd failed. As I got into Dad's car with Jeff, they both assumed I had made the team. Halfway down the Van Wyck Expressway, I told them the bad news. They were in shock, and I put on a brave face for the ride home. They might have asked me questions during that ride, but all I could concentrate on was not bursting into tears. I told my mom when I walked in the door, and she was very nice to me, but I needed to be alone. I went up to my room and cried all night long. How do you handle rejection for the first time in your life? No one talked to me about what I needed to work on, and it was very harsh. The next day at school, I immediately went through the list and saw players who I was better than, rationalized that I'd made it to the last cut, I tried my best...blah, blah, blah. The truth was, I wasn't that good, and that was the bottom line. After a couple of weeks, I decided with the help of my parents that this rejection was going to drive me to become a better player, and I was going to make the junior varsity next year. Rejection and failure can teach young people valuable lessons. I learned at age fourteen that I needed to get better and compete at a high level to play at Molloy. It wasn't until my high school coaching career that I realized that I hadn't deserved to make the team.

Our varsity team won the Catholic City championship in 1987, and they had a stacked team, led by sophomore All-American guard Kenny Anderson. Archbishop Molloy was in the top twenty-five of the USA Today high school rankings. Anderson was surrounded by future St. John's Redmen center 6'11" Rob Werdann, and Molloy's valedictorian and team captain, Ralph James at forward (Harvard). The two other starters were 6'10" Kevin McBride (Fordham) and 6'3" guard John Dunne (Ithaca). Molloy was stacked in a Catholic League that was talent-packed. It would be an honor to play for Coach Jack Curran and this proud program.

In the spring of my freshman year, I made friends with Eamon Howley and Andrew Huang. They were two great kids from Jamaica, Queens who loved to play pickup basketball games in schoolyards to compete. They added me to their three-on-three team, and we became a tough team to beat. I spent a lot of time going around Queens with a chip on my shoulder, trying to prove to everyone that I could play ball.

The summer going into my sophomore year, I went to Jack Curran's basketball camp at Fordham University for two weeks, practiced and/or played every day, and grew three inches to 5'9". I was motivated, bordering on obsessed, to make the JV. In sophomore year on the first day of school, my chances went down, as 6'6" Pat Cosgrove transferred in from the closed-down St. Agnes on Long Island. I went up to him immediately and sarcastically asked him if he played basketball. Pat smiled and said very simply, "Yes."

Pat was a man of few words, but we were instant friends. I went home and re-figured my spot on the team. I had a list of who was going to make it, who was on the fence, and who would get cut. I was on the fence, but still felt very confident going into the October tryouts.

In the fall of 1987, I made a connection with my religious education teacher. His name was Brother Ron Marcellin, and he was a Marist Brother, but he didn't wear a robe like the other brothers at Molloy. Br. Ron was a rebel from the 1970s who used rock music to teach lessons of peer pressure and decision-making. He loved playing Billy Joel and Meatloaf songs, and asked us to relate the lyrics to teenage issues such as drinking, drugs, and sex. I felt comfortable in his class to express my feelings in a peer setting, because Br. Ron was so understanding. He had a great ability to build up your confidence.

I still remember the days leading up to tryouts. Everything felt right. My freshman year social studies teacher, Mr. Sutter, was the coach, and we had a good relationship. My mom had bought blue and white towels for me in case I made the team. I was in great shape and playing on another level. This was the year, and nothing was going to get in my way. I was going to play great defense, make my open shots, and hustle like I always did.

Saturday morning in late October came, and I got on the bus with my Walkman, Van Halen cranking in my headphones. As I walked below Queens Boulevard at the Van Wyck subway station tunnel, I felt confident and fired up. As tryouts started, I was on fire. I remember my new friends Gene Devine and Joe Burns coming up to me and saying that I'd done well. My game was on another level, so I thought things were going well. Day two went the same way, and Coach Sutter explained to us that he was going to bring back twenty players on Monday for a last look. I was on the list, and my friends Joe Burns, Gene Devine, and Eamon Howley were as well. That Monday, they put a freshman guard on the JV named Jeremy Livingston, a nice young man and a great player. If he was on JV, that was one less sophomore, and every one of us was nervously excited about Monday's afternoon tryout. That school day was brutal. I don't think I learned a thing that day because I was so focused on basketball. The tryout came and went, and Coach Sutter said he had some hard decisions to make, but would try to take as many as he could. He would put a list on Coach Curran's door early Tuesday morning. That was one of the longest nights of my young life. I didn't sleep much, and I had some doubts. I got to school just in time for my first period class, and saw Eamon in the hallway. He had a sad face, and I asked what happened. He said he made it, but that I should look at the list after first period. My stomach dropped and that awful feeling from freshman year overtook my body. I wanted to leave school, but I sucked it up until later. I saw Pat Cosgrove and Joe Burns at lunch, and they were shocked I hadn't made it. Eamon felt so bad, he didn't even bring it up. I don't know how I made it through that day, but I was absolutely devastated.

I was able to speak with Brother Ron late in the day, and he was awesome. He let me know that this was just a temporary setback, and I should keep working on my game if I truly loved basketball. He had a way of looking at the bright side of every situation, and really gave me a confidence boost by mentioning that I was an outstanding young man. That's the only thing that really matters in life. I look back now and must say that Ron was absolutely right.

When I walked in the door that afternoon, my mom was in shock, and she didn't know what to say. She said she would offer to speak to Mr. Sutter, but I asked her not to—maybe I would in a couple of days. She had already made my favorite meal, chicken cutlets, but telling my dad again was going to be difficult. This was a man who got up every morning at 4:30 AM and worked seven days a week for twenty years. I was afraid to tell him because he was always positive and supportive with me. He also felt, as I did, very confident that I was ready to make the team. Angelo was an all-star in high school at Erasmus in Brooklyn, and he always excelled in sports. I was now a two-time loser, and felt bad that he would have to tell his friends that I got cut. How would I tell him? As he came in the door, my mom gave him a look that I was upstairs, and he came up to talk.

What happened next was extremely important to me.

The first thing that my father said was, "How are you doing, Bill?"

I started to cry and he held me. I stuffed my face in his shoulder so I wouldn't have to make eye contact. My father sat me down and said, "Bill, don't give up on your dream of playing basketball in high school or college. So what, you were cut from the JV, big deal. As long as you give it your best and get better each day, you can achieve your goal."

He continued, with a positive emphasis, "You're a good player, and when you get taller and stronger, you'll be able to make the varsity, and you WILL play college basketball."

I was thinking to myself that he didn't get it. You don't make varsity at Molloy unless you play on the freshman or JV teams. But looking back now, he was trying to tell me that you never let someone tell you that you can't do something. "Can't" is a negative word that only losers use. I appreciated his positive attitude and undying support. And once again, my father was there when I needed him. The reality of going to a school like Archbishop Molloy was that I had no chance of making the varsity team as a junior; he knew it and so did I.

CHAPTER TEN

FAILURE CAN BE A POSITIVE MOTIVATOR

MY SOPHOMORE into junior year was eventful. It was the spring of 1988, and I was finally feeling better about myself. My life was going to school, playing hoops after school somewhere in Queens, and doing my homework. That was it, but Molloy had a big-time dance each month, where girls from all over NYC would come and take over our gym. I would usually "hold up the walls" with the rest of the freshman and sophomore classes, but this night was going to be different. I was going to dance with a girl, no matter what! It had been two years of high school already, and I hadn't spoken to a girl. I look back now and realize how wrong that was. As a teacher, I see why boys and girls should be in school together. It's vital to their social development.

Imagine a sixteen-year-old boy in high school who has not seen or talked to a girl for two years. The built-up hormones had made me go all out at the last Molloy dance. Joe Burns and myself stepped up big time. Joe was an extremely confident Rockaway guy who had a way of making you feel like the greatest person on Earth. We became friends during our sophomore year, and on this night, he had a plan. We moved from circle to circle of girls, but we were given what my group of friends called "the Heisman Trophy," which means the push away. For two hours, we walked around that gym and tried to get into a circle of girls. That's how girls danced back then, in circles to protect each other from losers like myself. I really had no clue how to talk to girls, and fail we did.

At the start of basketball season in my junior year, I did something that, looking back, was pretty important to my development as a basketball coach. I had no shot of making the varsity team as a junior, so I asked Coach Curran to be the manager of the team, and he said yes.

Let me start by describing Coach Jack Curran. He was a legend in New York City basketball around the time I was born. Coach Curran was an outstanding baseball and basketball coach at Molloy, but could come across gruff and stubborn. I liked speaking with him whenever I could, because he always asked my opinion on things regarding sports.

My relationship with him, as his manager, was different than other students at Molloy, and because of that, we became close as I got older. When I was a high school junior and senior, I didn't realize the coaching internship I was about to receive. First of all, he gave me enormous responsibilities that make me shake my head when I look back now. I was responsible for the scoreboard during practices, filling in as a player/coach on certain drills, and doing the scorebook for all games. I was also responsible for compiling all of Kenny Anderson's 2,621 points, which was a New York state record in 1989. We traveled to a showcase in St. Louis and the Beach Ball Classic in Myrtle Beach that year. I met big-time Division One college basketball coaches like Bobby Cremins of Georgia Tech, Dean Smith of North Carolina, Jim Boeheim of Syracuse, and Louie Carnesecca of St. John's.

Answering Coach Curran's phone was a task in itself. From 2:30-4:00 p.m. every day, if Coach Curran wasn't in his office, I had to handle calls from all over the country. In the 1988-1989 basketball season, *USA Today* had us as a top team in the country. Dave Krider, who has covered high school basketball for over thirty years, would call my house every Sunday morning at 9:00 for an update on our team and Kenny Anderson's stats. Kenny would end up being the Daily News player of the year in New York City, New York state coaches' player of the year, and more impressively, Gatorade player of the year in the U.S. I was given a firsthand look at how to run a practice, how to handle substitutes, and how to manage different personalities.

I also blossomed as a player. On my CYO team at St. Joseph's in Hewlett, we had a good team that included Eamon and Jeff from Molloy. But Jeff was going through a tough time because his mom had just died and his dad left him. So Jeff was living with a bunch of different people off and on, and then finally lived with his brother out east. The Marist brothers at Molloy took good care of him in his senior year.

This CYO league was a great release for all of us. We played great all through the season and rolled to the Nassau/Suffolk championship at Chaminade HS. I was so pumped to play in front of a crowd and get a chance to win a championship. We started slow as a team, but we were in the zone. Eamon and I were hitting jumpers and playing great defense. Jeff took over the second half and we never looked back. What a great feeling to be a part of a championship team! Some of the guys on the team invited us all back to Valley Stream for a victory house party. I was starting to feel socially comfortable, and basketball became the center of my world.

As the summer before my senior year was in full swing, I became very close with Pat Cosgrove, Joe Burns, and Joe Grimpel from Molloy. All of us played basketball, but only Pat "Coz" played on varsity. The four of us would have two-on-two battles all the time, and that would continue for years to come. We all attended Coach Curran's camp at Fordham again, but there was a change for me. I was selected to play in the big all-star game with Division One players on the main court on the last day of camp. This was a huge boost for me. I had never played that confidently before.

Joe Burns would invite us down often to his house in Belle Harbor, NY (which was a section of Rockaway Beach) and we would have a blast. Joe's parents, Big Joe and Aunt Audrey, were great hosts. In the summer of 1989, I was able to play in the St. Francis de Sales summer league, and I was put on the same team as Joe Grimpel. We won the high school league that summer and had good times at the Burns' beach house in Belle Harbor.

Senior year came, and I was now 6'1" tall. I was very confident in my skills, but even more as a person. I felt like I'd matured and was ready to try out for varsity, along with Joe Burns and Joe Grimpel. Coz was going to be a star, but Joe and Joe were in my boat now. We had realistic expectations of maybe not making the team, but I had the job of team manager to fall back on. Tryouts came in late October at Queens College, and Coach Curran pulled me aside to tell me something that I didn't want to hear, though it was true. Now that I'm a varsity coach, I see where he was coming from. I knew there were four Division One guards in the junior class.

Coach Curran said in his brutally honest way, "Billy, I can't use you on the team, but I need you to be our manager. You can practice with us every day. I will need you in drills." I was heartbroken because I had improved during the summer, making the all-star team at Curran's camp, and nothing else mattered to me more than wearing a Molloy uniform. I wanted to follow in the footsteps of decades of great players whose pictures decorated the walls in the Molloy locker room. When I told my parents, who expected the news, they told me not to give up, and it was my dad who said I could still play college basketball. To be honest, my hopes were becoming slimmer. My parents were always very positive and supportive, but my realistic side did start to show up. Looking back now, I had improved to the point of playing for any team in the city, with the exception of Molloy and Christ the King.

So I sucked it up and took the job as manager/practice player. Burns and Grimpel didn't make the team, like a lot of the players in our senior class. Only four players from our grade made the twelve-man roster. Our juniors were excellent, but we felt at the time that Coach Curran could have added two or three more players. Anyway, I gained valuable experience playing against the starters as a "pinny." According to Coach Curran, a "pinny" was a player who knew his role as a practice player and sat the bench. We had a group of pinnies that played hard every day. I guarded our best scorer, junior Steven Frazier, who eventually played four years for Miami. That year of basketball made me a better player, especially for CYO. But still, no uniform for me at Molloy. This put a huge chip on my shoulder, and I used it to my advantage.

Once again, we travelled to Myrtle Beach, South Carolina, to defend our Beach Ball Tournament championship, like in the 1988-89 year. Our team was balanced, a lot different than the Kenny Anderson squad from the year before. We had Pat "Coz" Cosgrove as our senior leader, as well as juniors Steve Frazier, Jason Gilliam, Jeremy Livingston, and John Mavroukas. All five players had Division One talent, and we played team basketball. No one standing around waiting for Kenny Anderson to create a play like last year. We faced Grant Hill of South Lakes, Virginia in the second round, and Coz played outstanding basketball. We won a close game and advanced to the championship, where we defeated Loyola High School of California, who had their own group of Division One players. After our big win, and right before the dunk contest, Pat Cosgrove was named Most Outstanding Player of the tournament over Grant Hill. But Grant had an announcement of his own. He grabbed the microphone after winning the dunk contest and told the crowd that he'd accepted a scholarship offer to attend Duke University. That made Duke the favorite to win the NCAA championship, due to his addition to a team that already had Bobby Hurley Jr. and Christian Laettner. Pat will always have Myrtle Beach to look back on and smile.

There was one game of note in February where I made an impact, at home vs. Xaverian High School. Brother James Vagan was and still is the scoreboard operator at all home basketball games. He asked me for a special favor late in the season. He had the opportunity to go to a Rangers hockey game against the Islanders at Madison Square Garden, so he asked me to do the clock for the varsity game. I agreed to do it with Coach Curran's blessing. This was also a big night for my friend Pat Cosgrove, as Joe Dunleavy, assistant coach of Hofstra, was there to offer him a college basketball scholarship after the game. Coach Dunleavy and I had a bond: both of us had worked as a manager for Coach Curran.

This was a big matchup for a high playoff seed in the Brooklyn-Queens division of the CHSAA. The game went back and forth, with both squads playing unselfish basketball. Xaverian was down two points with the ball at the end of the game and hit a basket with one second left on the clock. Coach Curran called timeout and stared at me as the players entered the huddle. He had an intimidating and scary look on his face. I'd seen it before and I knew what he wanted me to do. He wanted me to hold the button until a Molloy player got a shot off. As that happened, the two referees came to the bench to explain how I would turn on the clock. The lead official told me to only look at his hand and nothing else once the ball was thrown in. When his hand went down to his side, that's when I'd hit the button. I was conflicted and nervous, to say the least.

Coach Curran sent out his team and gave the ball out of bounds to John Mavroukas, who would throw the long pass. John was a muscular player, with the strength to throw it to big Pat. The crowd was on their feet as the ball was thrown to midcourt to Pat Cosgrove, just like Coach planned. He caught the ball, pivoted to his right, and launched a desperation half court shot. The buzzer went off before the ball left his hand, and the ball went in! I ran onto the court with the players to celebrate, but the referees came to the scorer's table to wipe off the basket. Coach Curran started arguing with the officials, even though he knew they'd made the right call. The game went to overtime, but junior sixth man Jason Gilliam took over the game and we won easily.

After the game, I went into Coach Curran's office to talk with assistant coach Fran Leary and Joe Dunleavy from Hofstra. As I walked in with the game clock, Coach Curran ripped me to pieces.

He yelled, "Billy, why didn't you hold the button longer? What the hell were you thinking about? Where is Brother James? He would have done it right!"

I probably shouldn't have said anything, but I felt like I had to respond. "Coach, I knew what you wanted, but the refs were looking at me. What could I do?"

Coach Dunleavy interjected, "Coach, Billy did a great job and you won. Everything worked out."

Fran Leary patted me on the back and said, "Great job, Billy. Can you get Pat so he can talk to Coach Dunleavy?" I left the room, and Coach Dunleavy followed me into the hallway. He grabbed me and said, "Billy, do you know how many times Coach yelled at me in my two years as manager? Don't worry about a thing, you did everything right. He's not mad at you. Do me a favor and get Pat. Bring him to Coach Curran's office. I want you to be there when I offer him a scholarship."

I felt better when Coach Dunleavy said that to me. He was very good to me, because we had that common bond of working for Coach Curran.

Molloy finished 21-5 and lost in the CHSAA quarterfinals to All Hallows High School. I played as much pickup basketball as I could in hopes of still playing in college. Fran Leary always looked out for me. He's a great coach, and he has always been very positive. There was also a young assistant at Molloy during my senior year named Norm Roberts who would say to me that I could play at the next level. He would help coach the pinny team at Molloy, and he was always around after the season to drive us up to his alma mater, Queens College, to play pickup games. (Coach Roberts is currently an assistant coach at the University of Kansas.) When he said I could play at the next level, it was nice to hear it from an adult other than my parents. This drove me to do some research about state university basketball programs. My father and I drove up to visit SUNY-

Oneonta and Plattsburgh. We met with the coach at Plattsburgh, and he was very nice. He did not guarantee me a spot, but said he would give me a solid look since I'd gone to Molloy and had driven eight hours to meet him. So after my graduation in June, I put my deposit with Plattsburgh, and my dream to wear a uniform for a varsity college team stayed alive.

Every spring, my mother told me to get a job. Working at Green Acres Mall was becoming a habit. It was a fun place, but you got paid nothing. I got a job working at a greeting card store and so did Pat Cosgrove. I was able to get him a job as a cashier, and in return, he would drive me everywhere. Little did I know that the greatest night of my high school career would take place after graduation.

CHAPTER ELEVEN

PORTLAND, OREGON?

THE SUMMER of 1990 was amazing. We graduated in early June and the party began. Graduations, beach parties in the Rockaways, and trips to a water park called Action Park in New Jersey. My friends and I were going to take advantage of every minute we had left together. Yet I felt a little uncomfortable talking about college with my friends, because I wasn't going to a private school. My family did not have the money to afford a big university, so the SUNY system was my best bet for a solid education. Wake Forest University, Hofstra University, Manhattanville College, Fordham University, Catholic University, Fairfield University, and Scranton University were all schools my high school buddies were going to in the fall. I didn't put a lot of time into the college search, but thankfully, my mother stayed on top of me. She was my driving force pushing me to better myself academically. Little did I know that a night after graduation from high school would determine my future education.

At noon on Tuesday, July 10th, I received a phone call from Joe Grimpel daring me to blow off work so he could have the pleasure of beating my summer league team in the St. Francis de Sales Summer Classic. This tournament is still around today, and has always drawn the best talent from NYC and Long Island. He'd been my teammate the summer before, and as much as Joe and I were friends, we were extremely competitive. I called work and asked to switch with the other stock boy, and he agreed. Thank goodness Joe Grimpel called me to talk trash, because I really needed the money for college. I had planned on not going to my game.

July 10th was one of those magical days. I left for the Rockaways with Coz and Pat Hurley as we spent the afternoon on the beach with Joe Burns, Joe Grimpel, and Mike Gillespie. While we were eating lunch, a seagull crapped on my head and shoulder. Everyone laughed and screamed as I looked up to the sky. I jumped into the Atlantic Ocean and cleaned up, then had a nice laugh when someone told me it was good luck.

Whenever any of us had a night game, the whole crew would come down to see us play, and then we would meet up at Joe Burns' house afterwards. The plan was to go to a beach party after the game with our crew. But when the 7:00 game time came, nothing mattered except winning. My team that summer was a great group of Molloy guys who'd never played varsity. I had a blast playing that summer with one of my very good friends, Mark "Boomer" Turner, along with Billy Egan and one of my favorite point guards of all time, Christian Stathis. Christian's dad was our coach, and he was great to play for because he wanted us to run, gun, and have fun. The game was tight, but we took over late and won 41-39. I had 21 points and Grimpel had 18. It was always fun to see him lose because he got so angry. Mike Gillespie had no problem letting him know, either, with his infectious, cackling laugh. I was leaving the court to talk to our friends when Joe Burns pulled me to the side.

With a serious look on his face, he said, "Bill, there was a college coach with Bugsy [the summer league director] and Charlie at your game, and they were talking about you." I thought Joe was pulling my leg like always, but before I could turn my head to look, Charlie Marquardt asked to speak to me. He was a young coach in our summer league (and is currently the head coach of Molloy College on Long Island).

"Hey, Billy, you played really well," Charlie said. "Congrats on the win."

"Thanks, Coach, I appreciate it."

Before I could continue, he interjected, "Billy, I'd like to introduce you to Coach Graffam, my college basketball coach. He's here in New York recruiting for his school."

He walked me over and I met one of the most important people in my life, Jim Graffam. Coach Graffam had an intense look on his face, with a strong build, and he was fired up about how I'd played the game.

Coach Graffam said, "Hey, Billy, my name is Jim Graffam and I'm the head coach and athletic director of Westbrook College in Portland."

"Thanks, Coach. Great to meet you, but excuse me...Portland, Oregon?" I asked.

He laughed. "Sorry, Billy. Portland, Maine. It's the largest city in Maine. I'm starting a new Division Three men's basketball program at a school that's going co-ed after 150 years of being all girls."

"Westbrook has 500 girls and about 25 guys on campus," Charlie broke in. "Pretty good odds, right, Billy?"

I laughed, and Coach Graffam asked where I was going to college next year.

"I have a chance to go and play at Plattsburgh State," I replied.

"Not anymore, you're not," Graffam said with absolute confidence. "You're coming to play for me at Westbrook College."

My heart was racing. He'd gotten me fired up about being part of a new program and actually playing! He liked an uptempo style, and pointed out a play in my summer league game where I got five offensive rebounds on one possession and finally scored. I was, in his words, "his type of player, someone who won't quit."

Coach Graffam told me about the million-dollar facility they were building for the upcoming season. Wow! He gave me a brochure (which I still have today), as well as some more information about the school. He wanted me to visit next week. I agreed to call him in two days after speaking with my parents.

We shook on it, and he then said in his thick Maine accent, "Billy, you're the right type of person for our program, so please think about what we talked about." He wanted good people with high character, and someone who had the courage to be a part of something new and exciting.

I walked away with the biggest smile on my face and told my friends, who were so excited for me. This was the best feeling I'd ever had. My friends were there to watch this, but now I had to get home to tell my parents. I was going to shower at Joe's and then hang out on the beach with my friends, but now I needed a ride home. I decided not to sleep at Joe's so I could tell my parents the great news. My mother had always taught me to go with my instincts and trust my gut. Coach Graffam made me feel a part of something, and I had a great feeling about Westbrook. I told Joe and our crew that I was going to get a ride home.

I couldn't believe that a coach wanted me to play college basketball. When I got dropped off, I sprinted to my parents' bedroom door. My mom was awake and she was surprised to see me. I told her about my night as my father slept quietly. My mom was excited for me right away, because she loved New England and the campus brochure looked beautiful. My dad woke up and we talked about the cost, my deposit with Plattsburgh, and visiting Westbrook. I finally fell asleep around 3:00 a.m., and the feeling I had was second to none. After a couple of days, my dad was on board because he trusted my gut feeling. It was important to have their approval, because I valued their opinions so highly.

I had a game two days later against Charlie's stacked team, and I played with energy and pride I never knew I had. This team was young and extremely talented. Jason Cipolla was a future star at Christ the King High School and played guard for Syracuse University in the 1996 Final Four. Another young player on Charlie's team was John Wassenbergh, who moved up to Maine to play at South Portland High and became a Division Three All-American at St. Joseph's College of Maine. Jason and John were budding stars. We lost a close game that night, but Mr. Stathis noticed a difference in my game. I was confident and powerful. Charlie came up to me and told me that I was a college player, and I was going to do great at Westbrook. He was a big influence in my life. Now it was time to visit Maine.

A week later, I visited Westbrook College with Sean O'Rourke, a Molloy classmate of mine, and his mother. Also along for the ride was one of the most intense competitors I'd ever played against in summer league. His name was Bernard Soto, but his nickname was Beanie (I still don't know why). Anyway, Sean's mom agreed to drive us to Portland to visit. Beanie and I sat in the backseat with Sean, and his mother and little sister sat up front. It was a long trip, but we were so excited to see what the future had in store for us.

We got to campus, and we were sold as soon as we saw the school from the street on Stevens Avenue. Maine is a beautiful part of the country, and Coach Graffam was telling the truth about us loving it. We met Coach Graffam at admissions, and there was a sign, balloons, and a tour guide ready to bring us around. Everyone we met smiled and welcomed to us to Westbrook College with a thick Maine accent. When you're from New York City, common courtesy is a little weird, but we smiled back and thanked them. We took the tour, and Graffam saved the gym for last. Coach Graffam was a great recruiter and knew the gym was close to being finished. He told us that this was going to be a special place for us. Coach then took us to Pat's Pizza down the block. He told us how great we were over and over again, and how much fun playing college basketball would be here in Maine. Coach spoke of another Rockaway player coming to Westbrook to visit. His name was Paul Peterson, and Sean and Beanie knew exactly who he was. They liked Paul and felt he would be a good fit. Plus, he was 6'7".

After the visit, we checked into the hotel, and my roommate

Beanie and I rented a video basketball game and played all night long. We bonded instantly, singing rap songs that we knew, making up stupid nicknames for NBA players, and talking about Westbrook being taken over by two kids from NYC: one from Canarsie, Brooklyn, and one from Rosedale, Queens.

When we got home the next afternoon, I met with my parents standing in my kitchen like always and explained that I was going to Westbrook. It was my decision to make, but I had to go to the bank and take out more student loans because it was twice the price of Plattsburgh. I couldn't care less because I was going to play college basketball. There was nothing more important than wearing a uniform, being part of a team, and getting a chance to prove to everyone that I could play.

I called Coach Graffam to let him know, and he was more than excited because all four of us were going. He sent me a summer workout and said I had to be in shape for September. I had no idea what being in shape meant, but it didn't matter in July. The rest of the summer was spent gearing up for my freshman year of college, and leaving was going to be hard. My friends from high school and my family were all going to be missed, but little did I know that the best was yet to come.

CHAPTER TWELVE

ONE OF THE BEST YEARS OF MY LIFE

IT RAINED VERY HARD the night before I left in late August of 1990, and it was fitting, because after a very tearful goodbye with Mom and Sis, Dad and I headed up to Maine. I packed very light: my clock radio, my mother's Peace Corps trunk filled with clothes, a blanket, and a pillow. At 6:00 a.m., we left Rosedale in Dad's silver Crown Victoria, and I looked out the back window from the backseat and noticed how dirty the roads were on the Cross Island parkway in Queens. I couldn't wait to get to Maine. Heading over the Throgs Neck Bridge, I fell asleep for the next two hours as we took 95 North up to Portland, Maine.

About six hours into the trip, my father and I stopped at a rest area and got out to stretch with hundreds of other families. I still remember how crisp the air smelled in New Hampshire at that I-95 rest stop. I had never seen a sky so blue, the way a sky looks after a big rain comes through the night before. It was fitting that there wasn't a cloud in the sky, because I was getting a fresh start and my life was about to change. The thought of the mystery ahead was exhilarating.

This is when Dad spoke to me for the first time about my future. We sat at a picnic table together and he said, "Bill, I'm so happy for you. You deserve the right to play college basketball, so take advantage of this amazing opportunity. It will be extremely difficult, don't let anyone take this from you."

I understood what he was saying. He had opportunities in college and did not take advantage of them. His biggest regret was not graduating.

We drove across the Maine Bridge, and I was so fired up. An hour later, we got off at exit 8 for Portland and pulled up to campus. What a sight! Students and cars everywhere. Balloons, banners, and welcome signs decorated the historic buildings. We parked in front of my dorm, Hersey Hall, and both of us gave a big sigh of relief. Dad helped me with my gear, moved me into my dorm room, and hugged me goodbye. He and I were not great with that kind of stuff; in fact, my family was never big on kissing or hugging, but this day was special. My dad had driven me seven hours up and was going to drive another six home. He is my hero. He rarely took off a day, he never complained, and he was very proud of my accomplishments. My father was so excited for me, and I appreciated him as well.

I showed up to a welcoming speech by the school President at the Ludcke Lecture Hall, and you could pick out the basketball team right away. There was Beanie, Sean, and Paul talking with the other freshman players. I introduced myself as we all sized each other up, as all men do, for playing time. We stood on the side and met with Coach Graffam. He was so happy to see all of us standing together. Freshman weekend had started, and we went over for dinner to the dining hall as a team. When I sat down with the other players, we scanned the room for girls, and there were a lot of them. Remember, I hadn't been to school with girls since the eighth grade. As I sat down with a giant Maine potato and some steak, I listened to this wacko across the table wearing a neon yellow hat backwards, covering his blond mullet, tell us about his fun living in Windham, Maine. His name was Andy MacVane and he was 100% backwoods, complete with the accent. To this day, he is the funniest person I've ever met. I also met Tom Landry, another farm boy from Maine, who seemed to have as many stories as Andy. They were like long-lost brothers. I must admit that the New York City guys, including myself, had some adjusting to do, but it was fun.

After dinner on that first night, we had orientation on each dorm room floor to get to know the other freshman students. We played a fun game where the resident assistant made us take off our shoes, blindfolded us, and made us find our own shoes. That was a fun activity because it really broke the ice. I was going to be sharing a floor with girls, when three months ago I'd gone to school with 1,600 boys. Anyway, it was good to meet everyone, and I was off to my single room by myself for the night. The reason I didn't want to party that night was my one simple rule: no drinking beer until after the season was over. I was going to condition myself as an athlete and be ready for Sept. 24 when our conditioning workouts started. That lasted two hours. When I heard the music blasting from the other dorm, I was over there partying like a rock star. I threw in a Rob Base cassette: guys and girls were dancing, drinking, and tasting freedom for the first time.

During those first three weeks of September, we would have workouts at local gyms because our gym was not ready yet. The ten to twelve players that lived on campus met the players who didn't live on campus. One afternoon after class, we played in the University of Southern Maine-Portland campus gym, and I met two new players. Ian Merrill and Ron Crosby were high school teammates at Portland High School. They had an edge to them, a toughness, that you noticed right away. Ian was a fearless power forward, and Ronnie was an excellent on-the-ball defender. Ronnie guarded me and gave me fits. We had a shoving match over a loose ball, and Coach Graffam pointed out that he wanted more fire like that on his team. As we got up off the floor, I noticed his Portland Bulldog tattoo on his right shoulder, right next to his mullet. The Maine guys loved the mullet hairstyle.

We had a basketball meeting with Coach Graffam a week before the season opener on September 24th. There were eighteen players at the meeting trying out for the team. This was a different coach than I had met during the summer. This was his first head job, and he meant business. He told us that not all of us would make the team, and that we would have to run two miles in under twelve minutes and thirty seconds to earn that spot. I was very cocky at that point, thinking that I was going to start every game and running the two miles was a joke. I was very wrong. Ted Quinn, our point guard who was a year older, showed us where we would run the two miles in the graveyard next to campus. In early September, I couldn't do a mile without stopping and holding my sides in agony. I thought I could show up for tryouts and do it on adrenaline. Boy, was I in for a big surprise.

Monday, September 24th, was a beautiful fall New England day, complete with bright sunshine and a nice cool breeze. Every one of the eighteen players stretched out in the graveyard together as Coach Graffam approached us in his pickup truck.

He stepped out and said, "I'm only taking fourteen players on the roster, so some of you are not going to make this team. This two-mile run will separate the men from the boys. If you don't make it today, you'll have to run it after my basic training every day for the next two weeks until you do it."

That hit me right between the eyes. I was nervous as I stepped up to the starting line for the first time. He yelled go and we took off. Ted Quinn and Jason Tupper took off like lightning, and that was no surprise, since they had been training every day. I tried to keep up, but I faded away. Beanie kept going, but I fizzled out with Paul Peterson, Andy MacVane, and a couple of other kids who stopped running. We finished in sixteen minutes, and only eight guys completed the two miles in under 12:30. Coach Graffam was fuming. He pointed to the high school gym across the street, where we would practice afterwards because our million-dollar gym was not quite ready yet. I think he was so pissed off that he thought we didn't deserve to work in "his gym." I can't say that I blame him, because we weren't in shape. Coach Graffam was a master motivator, and these next two weeks, which he called conditioning, we called "basic train-ing." As an army reservist for over twenty years, Coach Graffam knew the value of mental discipline. Over the next two weeks, he would put us through hell, and as for myself, it was as good as advertised.

Sammy Hagar, former lead singer of Van Halen, once said, "I don't know what I'm doing, but I know how to get it done." This quote made a lot of sense to me at this time in my life. I was clueless about my life, but I enjoyed every moment. I can't put into words how hard we worked each practice, but it was more exhausting mentally than physically. (Who am I kidding, I would walk back to the dorm with a limp like I had been beaten with a baseball bat.) There's a reason why the military goes after eighteen and nineteen-year-olds. I could handle the 220-yard sprints in the street every other day, and the physical torture in the gym, but the constant criti-cism was wearing on me. By day five in the first week, three people had quit, and I was one of four players who hadn't finished the two miles yet. That put a huge target on my back, along with Paul, Sean, and Andy. Coach gave us an ultimatum: finish the two-mile run by the last day of the two-week conditioning program or be cut. We had to get this done. Luckily we had Saturday and Sunday to rest. There were no parties on campus that weekend.

Running two miles each day after our workout was torture, and on day six of the ten-day "Graffam Basic Training," Paul, Andy, Sean, and I went over to the graveyard next to campus. While we stretched, Coach drove over and said to "get it done" so we could get serious as a team. As he was walking away, one of the scariest things I have ever witnessed happened right in front of my eyes. An older man had just finished a run and was staggering toward us. He collapsed at our feet, holding his chest. A nearby dental hygiene student named Kristin Brown started CPR immediately, and Andy ran back to school to call 911. We watched in horror as this man gasped for air. They did all they could as a crowd formed around him. The EMS got there, but it was too late. The man had expired in a span of three minutes. I was in shock, to say the least, and puked behind a nearby tree. I had never seen a person die.

Coach Graffam gave the stopwatch to Ronnie Crosby and said, "I'm going to follow the ambulance to the hospital. Shake it off, boys, and get it done." This was Coach Graffam's motto. Find a way to overcome an obstacle and get it done. It was his way to be mentally tough in the military.

Paul, Sean, Andy, and I lined up and the two-mile run began. All I could think about was that poor man and his family. Thoughts of my own family and my mortality raced through my mind. Not to mention that we were running in a graveyard in Maine. This was setting up to be a Stephen King short story.

As we made the turn for the second mile, Ronnie yelled to us that we had a shot to do the two miles in under 12:30. Paul and I made eye contact and got to work. Sean and Andy decided to start walking three minutes before, but we were cruising. As we got near the finish, you could tell that we had some adrenaline working. We sprinted the last fifty yards and finished in under 12:30. Ronnie patted us on the back to congratulate us. Sean and Andy were the last two players to not complete the two miles; I was excited, but Sean and Andy only had four days left.

I couldn't get that man's face out of my head. I think I completed the two miles because I was thinking about someone else. I learned on that night how to focus when I was doing something competitive. It was clear as day, and from that time on, if I focused on something else while shooting a foul shot or hitting a softball, success would follow. Some athletes call that "being in the zone," but I call it an absence of concentration or focus. This has been an important tool for me over the years, and I still use it today as a coach.

CHAPTER THIRTEEN

MAKING HISTORY ON AND OFF THE COURT

ON THE LAST day of conditioning, Andy went down to the Portland Waterfront and knocked the two-mile run out of the park. He and Coach Graffam met before he ran, and for some reason Andy ran like the wind. Coach Graffam had a way of motivating us, and we bought into his philosophy.

Coach Graffam often spoke of the historical importance of our inaugural season at Westbrook College. He made reference to the opportunity that was given to us, that we should take advantage of this situation. He had no problem explaining to us that we were fourteen players who no one wanted, and our opponents would know that. We christened the Beverly Burpee Recreation Center in late October of 1990, and Joan Benoit Samuelson, who won the Gold Medal in the 1984 Olympics for winning the marathon, gave the welcome speech. I would spend a lot of time in this building over the next two years.

The Westbrook College gym was a sanctuary for me in my freshman year. Not only did I play basketball inside, but I worked for Coach Graffam for my work-study job. I felt so comfortable there because I was a part of something special. It was brand new and reminded me of a hospital, clean-smelling and white walls everywhere. The gym floor was made of composite rubber, not the traditional wood flooring, so it had a unique bounce and new smell to it. The locker room area was brand spanking new. We spent a lot of time talking about life in that locker room. Great teams can be created in locker rooms. It was a place where we complained about how challenging Coach Graffam's practices were. A place where we could be brutally honest and keep secrets. We had a bond where what was said did not leave the locker room. Most of the time, we were setting up where we were going to drink beer. Being together was extremely important to the fourteen freshmen who made the team.

We spoke often of the amount of running Graffam made us do. We thought we'd signed up for basketball, not cross-country. He was very tough on us, and we didn't know why. We get it now as adults, we were teenagers playing against men. Coach wanted our practices to be harder than our games.

Our practices were very challenging, but now that I'm a coach, I see that they were outstanding. Coach Graffam and Coach Johnson always had a plan, and I absolutely loved competing in practice. The drills were game speed and could be applied to every part of our game plan. It took us time to pick up Coach Graffam's energy and philosophy. Coach gave out a daily award for the hardest worker, also known as "player of the day," and each of us competed for his approval. That motivated us to be at our best each day. There would be parts of practice where we would break up the guards and forwards. I loved going to work with Coach Johnson and the big guys. He taught us post moves and footwork, and broke it down in a way we could understand. Coach Graffam would work with our shooters, and then after ten minutes we would come back together as a group. Graffam's practices made sense to me, and I use his practice methodology with my teams today.

It was a season of firsts. The first game, the first basket, the first win, etc. We played our first game in the Unity College tournament in central Maine in front of thirty people. I was so nervous, and it showed, as I missed every shot from the field. That was nerve-wracking, but I got that bad performance out of my system and played slightly better as I got more comfortable. Our first win took some time as we started the season 0-6, but conspicuously absent was our 6'7" center Paul Peterson, who found out he had testicular cancer at age twenty. This was horrible luck for Paul. Here's a guy who, like myself, never played high school hoops, was overlooked by everyone, got in great shape, but got cancer dealt to him? Why? No one knows why these things happen, but he handled it like a winner. Paul went through the entire conditioning program, and the doctor said it helped him recover so well after his operations. He was diagnosed in late October, and Paul was back playing after two surgeries in early December. What an inspirational story he was to us all; there was no secret to our success. We were lost and played so badly in those first six games without Paul. I started all six games, but I was completely overwhelmed. These were my first official games I'd ever played in a real uniform at any level. I had one good game at the University of Maine-Augusta, as I scored eleven points in a 96-89 loss at the Augusta Civic Center. The only problem was our defense. We were learning the help-side system, but it was going to take time. I will never forget the player I guarded that night. Dana Brann of UMaine-Augusta had 39 points on us (really me) because they ran the very methodical flex offense. They ran him off screens and we (me again) had no clue how to adjust to it. We had a lot to learn about help-side defense, but I felt like I was starting to understand it. Paul was rejoining us later that week, and even though we were 0-6, we were starting to feel better about ourselves. Coach Graffam's system of high-energy pressure defense into uptempo, unselfish offense was fun to play and great to watch. I learned the value of a coaching philosophy, physical conditioning, and player roles in my freshman year.

In Paul's return to action in the first week of December, we finally broke through with a blowout win over the University of Maine at Fort Kent. What a special night, as Paul's doctors had cleared him since he was in great shape before the surgery. We won a couple of games and then had to make a six-hour trip north to Presque Isle, Maine. When you played Division Three sports in the 1990s, there were long van rides, very little meal money, and no iPhones or personal computers. You really got to know your teammates and FM radio stations.

We got to the hotel in Presque Isle after six hours in a van, and the coaches let us go in the hotel swimming pool. This was a bad idea, as we took the pool over, and fourteen players absolutely beat the crap out of each other. The next morning, we woke up sore and exhausted. We played horribly at Presque Isle and lost. After the game, we drove two hours north to the University of Maine at Fort Kent. We were now going to the Canadian border, with all French-speaking radio stations. In Fort Kent, we went to a Subway sandwich shop for the first time in my life. On the walls of the sandwich shop, they had a mural of the NYC subway system. Here I am in Fort Kent, Maine, having dinner, looking at the E train line, and I didn't miss Queens at all. It didn't matter that I was eight hours north of Portland or that I was playing poorly. I was having a blast with a great group of guys and two coaches that I respected.

When we got back to campus Sunday night after an eight-hour ride home, Coach Graffam called me into his office. He sat me down and said, "Billy, you're not playing like you were four games ago. I'm going to make some changes in the starting lineup."

I was in shock, but I understood. I said, "Coach, I'll do whatever you think is best for the team."

He responded, "I appreciate your unselfishness, but aren't you mad that I'm taking you out of the starting lineup? That doesn't upset you?"

I replied, "Coach, I'm a team player. If you think coming off the bench will help the team win, I'll do it."

"Billy, you have to be more aggressive in games. You stand around and play scared. You instantly look to pass into Paul, and your help defense is poor. But you can work on those two parts of the game."

He then added this important point as he saw my head drop. "I know you can do more. Six months ago, no one wanted you, and now you have an opportunity to do great things at Westbrook. Where's that kid I saw in that Rockaway playground? Don't let someone take that opportunity from you." He realized that I was very sensitive, due to the fact that only two people in my life had said I really could play college basketball. As a teacher, he knew how to speak to me so that I wouldn't lose my motivation to help our team win.

Coach Graffam taught me in December of 1990 about personal pride and competitiveness. He excelled in getting the most out of each player. Coach Graffam replaced me at small forward with my good friend Beanie Soto. He replaced our point guard Teddy Quinn and our shooting guard Ron Crosby as well. Coach wanted to see if coming off the bench would motivate us. It did, but it took three or four games. It was nothing against my teammates, but I picked it up in practice and played much better for the rest of the season. That was a turning point for our team, as we went on a roll into the second half of the season.

The great thing about college basketball is the long layoff after the fall semester ends and the start of spring classes. For three weeks straight, we lived on campus alone and did nothing but work out twice a day. Lorraine McNerney was the best player on the girls' basketball team from New Jersey. She brought her teammates up to our dorm each night, and we threw dance parties in the hallway over Christmas break. Beanie Soto and I had a dance routine like the rap group Kid 'n Play that was a big hit. We had loud music, beer, and great friends. It was a great team bonding experience. I think we really came together during this time, and the parties were epic.

Andy MacVane had great ideas for team bonding. He was a likable person who had a way of getting everyone on board. In September, he took us to Windham for a great breakfast place called Chute's Café, followed by making us jump off a cliff named Frye's Leap into Lake Sebago. I never thought I had the guts to do it, but when I saw a six-year-old boy jump along with my entire team, I did it.

Andy had a big dorm room and invited the entire team to watch a television show on Wednesday nights: *Beverly Hills 90210*. This show wasn't exactly what a college basketball team would be known for, but we quietly all really liked it. We had popcorn made, the Mountain Dew was flowing, and no students were allowed in his room unless they played on the team. Sometimes one hour a week can bond a team; I never forgot that.

We reached a new height in mid-January of 1991, as we went into the University of New England tourney in Biddeford as a huge underdog. It was a four-team tourney for huge bragging rights in southern Maine. U.N.E. won easily in the first round, but so did our young, all-freshman squad Westbrook College, and the matchup was now here.

This was the tournament where I won my starting job back. I had the task of guarding their best shooter, and I locked him up. Paul had to sit out the first half due to his lateness to the team van, so others picked up the slack. We took a surprising ten-point lead, and big Paul came in for the second half. We had momentum, but we hurt the pride of U.N.E. and they made a nice comeback in the closing minutes. The score was tied, the crowd was yelling obscenities at our team, and we had the ball. Ian Merrill was a loyal and competitive teammate. Teddy Quinn took the ball to the basket and missed, but Ian grabbed an offensive rebound with two seconds left and got fouled shooting. He stepped to the line and swished the first one. The crowd went nuts, and the U.N.E. students started cursing at him. Merrill loved that stuff. He was a tough kid from the streets of Portland, Maine, and this was nothing new. He hit the second one and then gave them the middle finger running back on defense. They missed a halfcourt shot, and we celebrated on their home court like we'd won the national championship in early 1991.

In a typical week, we would play two games on the weekend against teams from all over New England. Two weeks after the

U.N.E. win, we traveled to Vermont on Super Bowl weekend. Coach Graffam was fully aware of Paul Peterson's devotion to the New York Giants. Since Paul was our best player and Coach knew he'd overcome cancer, Coach did something very humane. He asked the coach of St. Joseph's of Vermont to move the game to noon, as opposed to 3 p.m., so we could get back to Portland, Maine for the Super Bowl. We played inspired basketball, won the game, and drove home in four hours to arrive at 6:15. The four New Yorkers sprinted down to the Student Union to watch the Giants/Bills matchup. We got there in time to see Whitney Houston's rendition of the national anthem. Paul was fired up like I've never seen, and we ordered Domino's pizza for halftime. Our teammates would walk over to check on us, but the New Yorkers needed to be alone. The biggest TV on campus was in the Student Union. We enjoyed ourselves, and as we got to the end of the game, the four of us were starting to lock arms on the couch for good luck. With seconds to go in the game, the Buffalo Bills' Scott Norwood set up to kick the potential winning field goal—Paul, Beanie, Sean, and myself sat on the edge of our seats. When the kick went wide right, I will never forget the scene of Paul picking up Beanie and throwing him through the ceiling tiles above. We jumped up and down and danced for five minutes. No one else around but four New Yorkers in Portland, Maine, enjoying a year that no one could have scripted better.

On another road trip, we were returning to Maine from a game in New Hampshire, where we would travel in two vans. On days where Coach Johnson would recruit at high school games all over New England, he would drive directly to the game with his own car, so Coach Graffam would drive one van and an older player like Ted Quinn or Paul Peterson would drive the other. This night was different, because there was some bad weather in the area, and the roads were getting slick and dangerous. Coach Graffam had lots of bad weather experience, but Paul didn't. Coach's van was in front of us on a road in Exeter, New Hampshire when we hit a squall of snow. In our van was Teddy Quinn sitting in shotgun, Ronnie Crosby,

Beanie Soto, Ian Merrill, Andy MacVane, Tom Landry, myself, and Sean O'Rourke in the way back listening to his Walkman. Paul hit the brakes very lightly, but it was too late. We slid on some ice into a ditch in front of a used car dealership going fifteen mph. It was a terrifying twenty seconds of sliding down an icy road and crashing into snow. Thankfully, no one was hurt, but the sounds of Paul's deep "Oh no!" and Sean's "Yeah, let's do it again, that was fun!" are the two things I remember. We got out of the van and Coach stopped ahead of us to check on us. As we surveyed the van situation, a convoy of salt spreaders drove down the road to clean it up for the ride home. We were so mad that it came *after* we'd gone off the road. One of our teammates took pictures of us pushing the van back onto the road, and Teddy Quinn drove the rest of the way home.

In January of 1991, President George H.W. Bush announced that our nation would send in ground troops to the Persian Gulf region to protect the sovereignty of Kuwait. He threatened Saddam Hussein, and our nation rallied around our armed services. Coach Graffam was an Army reservist and had American flags put on our uniform jerseys in honor of the soldiers fighting in the Persian Gulf. There was talk of President Bush calling in the reserves and enacting a draft if we were to dethrone Saddam Hussein. This was scary, to say the least. Coach was fired up to be called into action if need be, but we had such a good thing going that we didn't want the season to end. Graffam was too young for Vietnam, and that had left a long-lasting chip on his shoulder. He wanted to serve his country like the other members of his family.

The perfect storm of illness and injury hit our team hard in early February of 1991. As we got ready to host Southern Vermont, point guard Teddy Quinn and his backup point, Robbie Brown, both were out with ankle injuries. Paul Peterson got food poisoning the night before the game, so we had to scramble to fill these valuable spots. I volunteered my services as point guard to Coach Johnson who, in turn, spoke to Coach Graffam on my behalf. They considered it, but felt shooting guard Ronnie Crosby would be better able to handle it.

But they put me on notice that if we needed help getting the ball up at the end of the game, I would be called upon. Andy MacVane would get a rare start at center in place of Paul.

It was a tight game throughout, and we were up four points in the last two minutes. I was called upon to break the pressure of Southern Vermont to help Ronnie. Andy was having a career game, and he and I had a connection. It was so easy getting him the ball in a position to score on the low post. But now we were being pressed fullcourt, and the other team was desperate for a steal and a basket. With a little over a minute left, I took the ball out under our basket. Coach Graffam wanted us to run our four across press breaker. He gave me the freedom to read the defense and the option to throw deep to Andy. I saw their pressure was tight and gave Andy a look. He understood my facial expression, and the referee handed me the ball. Andy gave me an amazing head fake and I threw it deep over his shoulder. He caught it in stride and made the layup as he was fouled. The crowd went crazy and I sprinted down to give Andy a high five. He hit the free throw and we went up seven points. Southern Vermont came down and hit a three-pointer to cut it to four points again. They called timeout with less than thirty seconds left. Coach gave me the same option as before, to throw deep to Andy depending on the defensive pressure. I couldn't believe the set-up of the Southern Vermont defense: exactly the same. I gave Andy a look, and he acknowledged me with a head nod, except this time he had his hands on his knees from exhaustion. But he smiled as he faked out his defender. Vintage Larry Bird-type move: Andy's favorite player.

The referee handed me the ball, and Andy's fake worked. Like before, I hit him with a long pass for a layup and a foul. I ran down the court, screaming, "I should be playing quarterback, Coach!"

He responded, "Geez, Billy, let's take it easy and win this game, please. Calm down, son." There was a big smile on his face.

I could not control myself. I was ecstatic about a win when we were short-handed, and I'd played a big part in winning the game for our team. Also, Andy finally got a chance to show how good he was, scoring 22 points and getting 16 rebounds in Paul's absence. I felt great after this win.

In our last weekend of games in mid-February, we had a chance to have a plus-.500 record with a win over the University of Maine at Farmington at home on Saturday and an away game at the Maine Maritime Academy on Sunday. Farmington was averaging 104 PPG, and our plan was to hold them to 95 points. We were putting up big scoring numbers as of late, so we were extremely ready to go. Coach Graffam had a way of setting short-term and long-term goals. Our short-term goal was to "outwork" them today, because today is the only day you can control. Even though we were 12-12 with two games left, this game meant so much to us. The night before the game, Coach Graffam informed us that there was a chance he would be deployed if President Bush were to attack Saddam in Baghdad. Beanie recalled later that Coach Graffam said, "Guys, don't feel bad for my poor family if I get deployed. Feel bad for poor Saddam Hussein."

That was his aggressive mindset, so we put together a warm-up cassette tape complete with Big Daddy Kane, 3rd Bass (they sampled JFK's inauguration speech from 1961 in their song), and finished with "Born in the USA" by Bruce Springsteen. It took us hours to find the songs and then record them onto a new cassette. Our manager, Woody Goodrich, had a sweet sound system to make the tape cassette. On Saturday, we put on the cassette twenty minutes before the game, and as time wound down, you could see Coach pacing quicker and quicker. As the song by 3rd Bass played and the words of President Kennedy blared from the sound system, "Ask not what your country can do for you, but what you can do for your country," Coach called us into the huddle with five minutes before the game. He grabbed a basketball tightly and said with authority, "It's clear to me that you guys are mentally ready. Let's get it done!"

We played inspired basketball as the score went back and forth. A bunch of freshmen sprinting, diving for loose balls, and finishing! The way Coach Graffam envisioned us playing. I remember scoring seven points in the second half as we took the lead late in the game. We had a feeling that we could get it done.

With four seconds left, the always-clutch point guard Teddy Quinn put in a layup to take a one-point lead, 95-94. We came into the huddle screaming and yelling. Coach reminded our all-freshman squad to keep their composure. We held them to 94 points, which was ten points under their average, but there was still four seconds left. Coach took me out to put in a taller teammate for the last four seconds. I wasn't upset, but I also felt that I was an excellent help defender, and I was not afraid to fail. All my youth, I'd played other sports like football and baseball, and defense was always my specialty. As Farmington took the ball out on the other baseline, their coach made a great move. He had his player throw a line drive to half court to a teammate, where he caught the ball and called timeout. I've used that coaching strategy at Hills West, and it works. Brilliant move, but now there were three seconds left and Farmington had the ball at half court.

I stood anxiously next to our awesome assistant coach, Mike Johnson, one of the most positive teachers and coaches I've ever had the pleasure to learn from. He actually listened to his players and used their input. Seconds later, they ran a backdoor, over-the-top lob pass to their best guard in the far corner, and he nailed a fifteen-foot jump shot to win at the buzzer. We couldn't believe it, and we were absolutely devastated. They celebrated on our court and we had to sit there and take it. We shook their hands and walked to the locker room, now with a 12-13 record. That was a silent locker room. But Coach Graffam was excited about the future of our program, and he knew we would learn from this for next year. And we knew we had to beat Maine Maritime on Sunday. His message was positive and uplifting. "Gentlemen, at the start of this season, no one gave us a chance of winning five games, and now we have a chance to go .500. I'm so proud of our program. Let's get a good night's sleep, we have to leave early tomorrow morning."

So what did we do after the game? Andy MacVane decides to

throw a keg party in his room in Ginn Hall. We felt that we were such polished drinkers that we would be able to drink all night, get up the next morning, drive to Castine, Maine, and beat them like we had early in the year. This party was legendary—the entire campus came out to enjoy. When the basketball team threw a party, everyone came to hang with us. We danced to LL Cool J, Rob Base, C + C Music Factory, and Vanilla Ice. A great time was had by all.

Getting up at 9:00 a.m. to drive in a van for three hours, play a game with a hangover, and then drive home sounds like fun when you're nineteen years old. But we needed to win this game to go .500. To no one's surprise, we played like crap, and Coach let us know at halftime. The game was close in the second half, but we were always in the lead. Up two points with ten seconds left, Coach called timeout to set up an inbounds play ninety-four feet away from the basket. Coach Graffam listened to Coach Johnson and kept me in the game for two reasons:

1. The coaches trusted me more than anyone to take the ball out. I'd never played a high school game, but averaged 4 PPG / 3 RPG / 3 APG, and in my eyes, I was the best passer on the team.

2. I was a 75% free throw shooter. We had our free throw shooting group in the game.

I was given the ball by the referee, and I passed the ball into Ted Quinn, our point guard. He was instantly trapped, and the other team had him pinned against the baseline corner. Ted got the ball back to me with five seconds left, and I was fouled. As I walked up the court to shoot my one and one, I looked up at the scoreboard and saw, "Westbrook 76 - Maine Maritime 74," and I overheard Coach Johnson say to Coach Graffam, "Graff, this game is over. Billy doesn't miss big free throws." I got to the line and set up my routine. Put my right foot on the nail in the middle of the foul line, took a deep breath, dribbled the ball three times like my favorite NBA guard Mark Jackson. That was my routine. I put my middle finger on the air hole of the ball, a trick that my dad had showed me years earlier. The first free throw was a swish. The other team on the foul line looked deflated. Westbrook 77, Maine Maritime 74. The opposing coach called timeout with the intent of icing me. That was the longest timeout of my life, but we didn't sit in timeouts, since Coach Graffam didn't believe in sitting. It made you look weak.

He firmly spoke in the huddle, "After Billy hits this free throw, just get back to the three-point line and don't foul!" Boom! All the pressure of this wonderful freshman year goes on my shoulders. My teammates were looking at me with quiet confidence, but they knew what this shot meant. If I hit this free throw, we win and go 13-13 with a group of freshmen playing veteran teams. All I kept thinking about was not letting down my teammates and coaches. Coach Graffam had taken me out of a summer league playground nine months ago, and now he was counting on me to "get it done."

As I walked onto the floor, Andy MacVane yelled to me, "Use your fat ass and hit this shot!" He always had a way of making me smile, as he must have seen my face filled with fear leaving the huddle. I got to the line, did my routine, and shot the basketball. It hit the back rim and they got the rebound with a chance to tie. I ran back to the three-point line with my teammates, and their best shooter got a great look at a three-pointer. The ball hit the back rim as Paul Peterson rebounded it and held on for dear life. Phew! I almost blew the .500 record. Coach Johnson told me in the van ride home that he'd bet the house on my foul shots. I apologized to him because he'd trusted me at the end of this game. He said, "Billy, I still want you on the line in a big spot next year. Keep working on your game." Coach Johnson had a way of always giving me support and confidence despite the situation.

We drove back to campus, and Andy still had beer in the ice-cold keg outside in the snow. We accomplished something no one could have imagined. To go 13-13 (after starting 0-6) with fourteen players under the age of twenty who never met before September. Playing Division Three basketball was extremely challenging, but rewarding beyond description. Our team got together in Andy's room and had a blast. Our motto was, "A team that drinks together, wins together." It would be the last time this group of freshmen would drink together as a unit, because changes were on the way. There's nothing better than helping your team win, especially when you're so close off the court. I finished the academic year strong, Duke upset UNLV in the NCAA Championship game, and I thoroughly enjoyed every minute of my freshman year.

In the summer of 1991, I went home and worked at Green Acres Mall again. Joe Burns got a job as a cabana boy at a beach club close by, and I was jealous. He was making $500 a week in cash tips, and I was making $4.25 an hour. I spent a lot of time with Joe, Pat Cosgrove, Pat Hurley, Mike Gillespie, and Joe Grimpel: "the Molloy boys." We weren't old enough to go to bars, so we spent a lot of time at Joe Burns' house in Rockaway or my backyard in Rosedale. Joe's parents, Joe and Audrey, were very hospitable, letting us stay over during the summer. We always had fun playing different sports, such as stickball and basketball. But I'd learned something valuable about offseason training last year. I made a goal to run the two miles in less than 12:30 on the first time. I did it in 12:23 my freshman year on day six. So I ran home from my job at Green Acres Mall every day that summer, about one and a half miles. I was not going to let a new recruit take my spot.

CHAPTER FOURTEEN

THE OPRAH

I LEFT for my sophomore year in Maine a new man. I was in shape, I was going to have my own dorm room, and I was going to be a leader on campus. Coach Graffam named me the student director of intramurals as my work study job. I couldn't wait for my sophomore year to begin. Some of my teammates didn't return due to grades, money, or family reasons. Only eight players returned out of the original fourteen.

Our new recruits were very talented, and we were going to be much improved. They were athletic, they could shoot, but they needed to go through the Graffam preseason conditioning program. Gary Kuhn was a shooting guard from South Amboy, NJ, and he was a great teammate. He lived next door to me and had a TV left in his room from the person the year before. He was nice enough to give me the TV. That was huge, especially since I didn't have one freshman year. Sophomore year was a lot of fun, but a lot less crazy. I didn't have a roommate for the second straight year. A group of players would come into my room to play cards every night and watch Johnny Carson and David Letterman. My weekday routine was simple. Class in the morning, then a quick nap around 11. Then more class, lunch, studying, and maybe an afternoon nap. Dinner from 5:00-5:30 and practice from 6:00-8:00. Shower, meet back at my room at 9 for cards, Key Food brand iced tea mix, and TV shows like *90210* and *Seinfeld*.

Coach Graffam had his way of creating a bond. When our conditioning stations began in late September, I was mentally and physically ready. We ran the two miles on Stevens Avenue this year, and I crushed the run with a 10:55 time. I cut over a minute off my time and did it on the first day. Everyone did it on the first day this year, including the incoming freshman. The reason was all the training I'd done over the summer, running home from Green Acres Mall four times a week. Something that simple went a long way in September.

"Basic training" seemed easier in my sophomore year. The running wasn't as bad, and the conditioning stations were better because Coach Graffam spent time breaking in the freshmen. He didn't spend much time dealing with the eight sophomores because he trusted us.

We only had twelve players in the 1991-92 season, so playing time would be plentiful. Coach Graffam's system was fast-paced and high energy, and it was fun to play and watch. He subbed players every four minutes, so there were plenty of opportunities to play. I got taller and stronger in the offseason, so he moved me from the wing to the power forward position. I was now coming off the bench, but I had an important role as a leader on the team. We loved his practices. Less than two hours, competitive drills, and always positive.

Halloween week in 1991 was memorable. We were a week away from our first game and had a scrimmage Friday, Nov 1st, but on the Wednesday beforehand I was taking my daily afternoon nap when a student named Bart knocked on the door. He was one of the few men on campus who didn't play a sport. He lived down the hall, and we would usually walk to dinner together with Gary next door. Bart's real name was Kurt, but we'd given him that nickname last year because he always wore a Bart Simpson shirt.

He knocked on my door and screamed, "Billy, wake up, man, hurry!"

"What's the big rush, Bart?"

"Open the door," he replied. "Did you just watch The Oprah?"

I was half asleep and stumbled over to open the door. "No, I didn't, Bart—I was asleep. Hold on, let me grab my basketball gear, and we'll walk to dinner."

Bart was visibly upset. He'd watched the 4 p.m. showing of Oprah, and told me that there was a psychic on her show predicting a mass murder on a college campus on Halloween in 1991 based on Nostradamus' writings 400 years ago.

"There are 20,000 colleges in the US, Bart!" I said.

"The psychic said the mass murder would take place on a campus on the east coast of the US, next to a body of water."

"Bart, now we're down to 5,000 colleges," I replied.

Bart continued, with fear in his eyes, "This is where it made me freak out. The psychic said they saw an L-shaped building on a college campus that was surrounded on one side by an army base and a cemetery on the other."

I looked to my left and saw the National Guard base next to my dorm, which was an L-shaped building. To my right was the grave-yard we'd run through last year. We walked into dinner, and the Westbrook cafeteria was crowded as usual for a Wednesday night. I sat down with the guys on the team, but no one was talking about Oprah. Some of the tables of girls might have been talking about it next to us, but I didn't give it another thought. We had practice at 6, and basketball was my focus.

After practice, some of the guys were coming over to play cards. We had a quiet night until the news came on and ran a story about the Oprah psychic. It matched the description of two schools in Maine, and Westbrook College was one of them. The other school was going to close until Friday, Nov 1st. We were laughing it off as total crap. At this point, we were indestructible, and no one would tell us how to live our lives. Especially since we had a scrimmage on Friday afternoon.

When I woke up for class on Halloween, I walked over to the dining hall for breakfast. There were a few people eating where you would usually see thirty or forty people. I went to class, and attendance was light. I walked over to the gym, and Coach Graffam needed me to work the home playoff soccer game after lunch. I was going to make twenty dollars to chase the balls on the sideline. I went to lunch at noon and met up with my teammates. There were about twenty-five people left on campus: the boys' and girls' basketball teams, and a couple of girls who lived too far away to leave. This Oprah-induced mass murder nonsense was getting out of control.

I worked the soccer game, then we had practice that afternoon. Coach Graffam warned us to do the right thing in the dorms, as we had a scrimmage Friday afternoon. We went to dinner after practice, and there were about fifteen people total on campus. Everyone else had left town. Our minds started to think about "what if?" We started to come up with crazy scenarios from horror movies, but the consensus was to stay together. I didn't have a roommate, so eleven players were coming over tonight. In looking back, though the college decided not to close, they should have done so.

We really didn't have a lot in 1991. Someone on the team had the idea to walk down to West Coast Video and rent a VCR, along with the *Halloween* movies: one, two, four, and five (we all agreed that *Halloween* 3 sucked). Paul had a credit card, so he used it, and we bought all kinds of soda and candy. All twelve players crammed into my room as Gary hooked up the VCR to my TV. We started the marathon around 6:30, and we were like ten-year-old boys at a sleepover. It was absolutely embarrassing, but we were together. Around 10:45, after *Halloween* 2, six of the guys decided to go to their rooms. Six of us remained. Big Paul had the beanbag on the floor, while Ronnie, J.P., Teddy, Merrill, and myself shared the double bed I had set up in my dorm room. When the other six guys left, Ronnie said he had to go outside to his car to get something. We thought for a second that he was going to get a knife or gun. That's how crazy we were getting. Our minds were racing, and we told him not to go, because that's how horror movies start. He came back to my room minutes later with three aluminum baseball bats. We absolutely made fun of him for that one.

Merrill, Ronnie's high school classmate, mentioned, "What are you going to do if someone has a machine gun? Block the bullets? You're a dumbass, Ronnie!"

That got us thinking about the military base outside my window. A disgruntled soldier gets angry...again, what if?

As we hit midnight, we were getting more childish watching the rest of the *Halloween* movies. Finally, at 2:00 a.m., the last movie ended in a cliffhanger and I asked the guys nicely to leave. One after another, they explained why they should stay over. So six college basketball players decided to sleep in my room, which was a little strange. Finally my giddy teammates decided to call it a night and fall asleep. Try to imagine five basketball players in two twin beds pushed together, and a 6'7" center on the floor, in a small dorm room. Try to imagine the amount of "what ifs" we'd gone through in the last eight hours. It was about 2:45 a.m., and the guys finally calmed down. The night was fun, and something we always talk about today.

According to Bart, on Oprah's show the next day, she said she was sorry for causing a problem for any colleges across the US. She wanted to start an urban legend, and nothing bad happened on Halloween of 1991. Our team really spent a lot of time together off the court in our first two years, and I found that even something stupid as watching horror movies can create a bond that translates onto the court. This is a bond we still share today.

We started off the season at UMaine-Augusta, where we'd lost by seven points the year before. Freshman shooting guard Gary Kuhn hit ten three-pointers and freshman wing J.P. Fennessey hit six three-pointers in a thirty-point win. We couldn't believe our eyes. Gary and J.P. had a gift for shooting, but you would never know it off the court. They didn't have big egos, and came to practice the next day and went to work. Paul was on his way to averaging a double-double in points and rebounds for the year. We had some big wins early in the season over teams we'd lost to the year before.

In December of 1991, we were invited to the Emerson College Tournament in Boston, where we faced off against Lyndon State, a team we'd lost to badly freshman year. Coach Graffam had a great method of substituting that made all twelve players motivated to play. Every four minutes, players were substituted to stay fresh, so we could play our high-energy defense into our uptempo running game. I was now backing up my very good friend Ian Merrill at power forward. He got into foul trouble against Lyndon State, so I was summoned to finish the first half. In the last possession of the first half, the ball was reversed to me on the left wing by Gary Kuhn, and I swished a three-pointer at the buzzer to take a seven-point lead. I sprinted off the court, with my teammates jumping on top of me as we went into the locker room. Coach loved when we finished on a good note so we could run into the locker room. He felt it would give us momentum going into the second half, something I would adopt in my coaching style later on. We started off hot in the second half as we kept the momentum going, but foul trouble caught up to us. Paul Peterson and Gary Kuhn had big games for us, but Lyndon State made a late run to keep it close. I was put into the game late, up four points, and I was fouled. Coach Graffam had confidence in me at the foul line late in games. I hit both foul shots, and we won 80-74 to advance to the championship game.

We'd given up 125 points to Lyndon State the year before, but held them to 74 this time. Coach made a big deal out of this point, to prove that our defense was starting to click in year two. We defeated Maine Maritime easily one day later and had a blast as a team that weekend. I accepted my reserve role immediately because Coach Graffam made me feel like an important part of the team. Coach made a point of my unselfish attitude after our tournament win. His positive energy and passion for our program made everyone feel worthwhile. We were getting better each day and gaining confidence.

We traveled down to Long Island, where Coach set up a game with SUNY-Old Westbury in early January. The night before our Saturday game, my mother cooked for the entire team and put on a feast that we thoroughly enjoyed. Our team was full leaving my house that night. Mom and Dad invited everyone in our family to see us play, and I played really well. But my mother didn't look good, and we spoke about the upcoming year. Mom sat me down and told me that my dad was going to need three minor surgeries this year. She also mentioned that she needed a small procedure done as well, so we needed to find a time in the next year to get them done. I didn't know how to respond. Were the surgeries serious? Did I need to leave school? What was the deal? She said we would discuss it next week on the phone. We lost on Saturday to Old Westbury, but it was great to see my family and friends. The next day, we travelled to Vassar College and won convincingly. Dad saw me play well once again. I felt good in my role off the bench. I spoke to my dad quickly after the game about how he was feeling, and he wouldn't say a word. He never complained, but only had positive words to say about my game and our team.

There were times in the season when I felt like a key contributor off the bench. I had two games with five steals that could be attributed to my knowledge of our help-side defense. Just being in the right position at the right time made it easy to steal passes. I worked with Coach Johnson every day in the post on my offensive moves. He was such a wonderful teacher, and I became a solid forward. Competing against Paul Peterson, Ian Merrill, and Jason Tupper every day made me a tougher basketball player.

Mom sent care packages with iced tea mix and cookies, and always included a written note. In her notes, she was dropping hints about her cardiovascular health, as well as my father's various maladies. You can learn a lot from the tone of a letter, and my mother was hinting at needing me around. When we spoke on the phone, she spoke of my father's sacrifice over the years for our family. He needed to get his gallbladder removed, arthroscopic knee surgery, and a cyst removed from his back. These would need to be done in the next year. In my mind, I felt an emotional pull back home from my mother. This was a dose of reality right in my face. How could I say no to my parents? My mother started to send me brochures for schools in NY.

We defeated highly ranked teams such as UMaine-Farmington and UMaine-Machias by holding both teams to twenty points less than their season average. Coach Graffam's defensive philosophy kept us in games our first two years, but now we had the offense to beat very good teams. It took time to teach, but our team bought in 100% to the "Westbrook Way."

In our last game of the season in my sophomore year, we traveled to Bates College at 17-9 with a chance to knock off a good team. We played well, but came up short, and after the game, I sat in the visiting locker room crying my eyes out. I knew in my gut that it was my last game at Westbrook. I hadn't made the official decision yet, but I knew deep down that I would not wear a Westbrook uniform again. Coach Johnson came up to me and asked if I was okay, but I couldn't tell him. He was pleased that I cared so much about our team. Coach Graffam and Coach Johnson had always been amazing to me, taught me the game with respect, and mentioned that I would join them on the coaching staff when I was done playing.

Telling Coach Graffam I was transferring was going to be heartbreaking. He was the only coach who'd taken a chance on me. When I had my end of the season meeting with Coach, he started by saying, "Billy, you did a wonderful job accepting a role off the bench, and I think we can make a jump to the national tournament with the recruits we have coming in next year."

I responded, "Thank you, Coach. I had so much fun this year. I think our team has a lot of potential in the future, but I have something to tell you. My mom and dad have to get surgeries in the fall, so I'm transferring back home to a school close by."

The look on his face went from relaxed to concerned. "Are your parents okay? Is it serious? I'm really sorry to hear you have to leave

Westbrook. You're an example of the type of person we want to recruit in the future. You do everything the right way, on and off the court. Is there a way we can make this work?"

"Sadly, I have run through all scenarios with my parents, and their surgeries will require me to take care of my sister for her senior year of high school. I'll lose the entire semester of school if I come back to Westbrook and then leave at the start of basketball season. That wouldn't be fair to anyone. I will most likely register at St. John's."

Coach stood up from behind his desk and gave me a hug. "Billy, you're doing the right thing for your family. You should ask Coach Carnesecca to become a team manager."

I smiled and said, "Good idea, Coach. I want to thank you for picking me out of that schoolyard in Rockaway Beach two years ago. You believed in me, and I can never repay you for that."

Graffam walked me to his door and said, "Billy, you will always be a big part of the Westbrook family. We will talk more during the spring."

The emotional pull I felt from home was extremely strong, and I was listening to my gut. But there was one highlight in the spring of 1992. March Madness is very special to me, and I spent the first four days of the tourney at home in my dorm room, watching as many games as I could. It was basketball nirvana for myself and my teammates. On Channel 6-CBS in Portland, they ran a promotion to play with the Washington Generals against the Harlem Globetrotters in mid-March. I sent in five postcards telling them about my dad playing for the Generals, and they chose me. Channel 6 came over to campus and did a promotional video with me in the Westbrook gym. Coach Graffam loved it because it really showed how great our school was to all of southern Maine. I played three minutes in the game at the Portland Civic Center in front of my friends. Dad was so proud of me following in his footsteps. The Washington Generals gave me a jersey and let me shoot as much as I wanted. I scored seven points in three minutes, but the experience against the Globetrotters was special. The following week, I went home for spring break and visited St. John's, where I spoke to admissions.

This move I was going to make was heartbreaking. In the two seasons at Westbrook College, I had set one record. I'd played in fifty-three consecutive games in our program's young history. Coming from the perspective of someone who never played a minute in high school, I'd just completed two full years of very competitive D3 basketball, and now I thought my career was over. Mom's health wasn't getting better, and I felt bad that I wasn't home to help. My father needed to get those minor surgeries done in the fall of 1992, so I had to make the biggest decision of my life. It was so hard, because Coach Graffam had taken me from obscurity to having a role and a purpose at Westbrook College. In late April, my grandfather Nick passed away, and I went home for the funeral. That sealed the deal. My parents scheduled their surgeries for late September, and I was to transfer to St. John's.

CHAPTER FIFTEEN

ALWAYS LISTEN TO YOUR GUT

AS I LOOK BACK TODAY, there's no question that the summer of 1992 was very tough, but also very rewarding. I got home from West-brook College after two fun-filled years of basketball and partying on my own. Reality slapped me in the face, as I had to get a summer job, buy a car, and live back home in Rosedale. This was a huge transition for me.

In May of 1992, as I made the move home, the Knicks (with Pat Riley at the helm), Patrick Ewing, Charles Oakley, Gerald Wilkins, Xavier McDaniel, Anthony Mason, and Mark Jackson made a run in the Eastern Conference playoffs, taking the Bulls to the brink before losing. It was great to see a tough and resilient New York basketball team. I enjoyed watching the NBA back then because it looked like the players really cared about staying with the organization that had drafted them. It was the start of a decade-long streak of excellence in the Garden. I must admit that I didn't like Ewing from Georgetown, but there's not one person more responsible for MSG being sold out for thirty years now than Patrick. The Knicks cannot pay him enough. (And I'm a St. John's fan!)

Speaking of St. John's basketball, in the spring of 1992, legendary head coach Lou Carnesecca retired after many years of excellence in Queens. He handed over the program to his longtime assistant coach, Brian Mahoney. I went to Molloy in June and asked Coach Curran how I should ask Coach Mahoney to be involved with the program. Curran said very simply, "Go into his office and ask him." Good idea.

Coach Curran had a very direct way of dealing with issues. I went in during the summer and asked Coach Mahoney to be a part of the staff. He was very nice and told me to go see his Administrative Assistant, Alex Evans. He's a wonderful person with a high motor. Recently, Alex has produced several 30 *for* 30 sports documentaries on ESPN. I spoke with him briefly, and he told me to come see him in October after the school year started.

In late May of 1992, as the Knicks lost to the Bulls, my dad put up $2,000 for a used baby blue four-door Dodge Diplomat that had also served as an undercover cop car at one time. I needed a car for my new summer job working as a locker boy at Sun & Surf Beach Club in Atlantic Beach, NY, which was about fifteen minutes south of Rosedale and just east of Rockaway Beach. I needed this car for school, too, because St. John's was a commuter school and a twenty-minute drive. The Dodge Diplomat was awesome. It had a V8 engine that cranked, and people all along the Cross Island Parkway thought I was a cop and got out of my way.

Let me try to describe a beach club. Unless you live in Long Island, California, or South Florida, you probably don't know what it is. Sun & Surf Beach Club was a unique place where members paid for privacy, service, and safety at the beach on the south shore of Nassau County. Members paid for accommodations, such as a beach locker or cabana to store their belongings and get changed. A great place to stay and relax for the summer. I was given the assignment of a locker boy, where I took care of sixty families with the task of bringing their chairs, umbrellas, coolers, and other items such as boogie boards and kiddie toys down to the beach. The great Joe Burns had worked there the summer before and got me an interview to meet with one of my future mentors, Jack Hubbard. He was the general manager and an excellent leader. Jack saw my size and ability to talk to adults and gave me locker section #3. Working lockers was a lot of hard work, but very rewarding. On any sunny weekend, I would bring forty sets of beach chairs, umbrellas, and coolers down to the beach in the morning, and bring them back up at the end of the day using a two-wheel wooden cart. Luckily for me, 1992 did not bring the greatest weather for the summer beach season. Ten of the twelve weekends had at least one rainy day. That meant a lot of slow days, but when it was sunny, I worked my tail off. It was a very prosperous summer. I was working the same amount of hours as I had at the mall in the summer of 1991, but wasn't making $145.00 a week anymore. I averaged $550.00 per week, and in the recession of 1992 to boot. Being a locker boy meant carting personal belongings about 150 yards in the sand and bringing them back up at the end of the day. Not only was I in great shape, but I learned how to talk to adults at age twenty. Whatever I could do to make their lives easier, I would do it. I got in trouble sometimes for playing football on the beach with the children of my members. More importantly, I always asked good questions and listened to them with a detailed mind. That was something my mom and dad taught me at an early age. To this day, I still remember the names of the people I helped out in 1992. I wrote everything down in a notebook for my relief locker boy so we wouldn't miss a beat.

My good friends from Molloy, Pat and Pete Hurley, would host late August parties, as their parents were away. All the guys came over to hang for days, and all we did was drink. One Friday morning, we got breakfast, played stickball, bought beer, and drank more. I played the rain game that Friday night. That meant I was going to drink a lot, stay up late, and pray for rain so I wouldn't have to work.

To my dismay, Saturday morning at 7:30 a.m., it was going to be 85 degrees and sunny. Ugh! That was a recipe for disaster with a hangover. My beach club buddies were in awe of my morning energy and ability to work despite the rough couple of days. I put my head down and went to work. From 8:30-2:30, I brought down forty-two sets of chairs, umbrellas, and coolers. It was a record for me. The busiest day of the summer, and I was hungover. At 3 p.m., I bought lunch, went down to the beach to an open area, and fell asleep in my cart. My body collapsed. One family was wondering what was going on, so I told them. They gave me a $100.00 bill and told me to get five piña coladas from the bar for us. They said I could keep the change, but they normally would get four. They winked and said one was for me. (Little did they know that I'd made friends with the bartender over the summer and he would make them for free for me, so I could keep the money after tipping him.) I got back to the beach and they made me sit with them until 5 p.m. Sunset was my favorite time of the day at the beach. There's nothing like it in the world. The sunset at a beach makes you feel good about being alive and makes all your worries feel insignificant. All I could think about was leaving Westbrook, and how my future was uncertain.

Pete Hurley and Gene Devine were the only people I knew at St. John's, and I went from a school with 500 students in Maine to 19,500 in Queens: big man on campus to anonymous. Thank goodness for Pat Cosgrove playing basketball at Hofstra, which was twenty minutes from my house in Rosedale. He included me in his crew and made my transition a little better. It was Labor Day weekend in 1992, and it rained all weekend long. I went into work for my end of the season tips and drove directly to Hofstra to drink with Coz and the basketball team all weekend. I drove to the beach club in a storm on Labor Day Monday, opened my lockers to leave my address in case people wanted to mail me a tip, and bought two cases of beer for Hofstra. We partied on campus, and I stayed over that night with two freshmen, Matt Carpenter and Chris Parsons. I woke up for my first day of classes at St. John's with a hangover. I drove forty minutes in rush hour traffic, couldn't find a parking space, couldn't find my classroom, and didn't recognize one human being on campus. It rained hard all Labor Day weekend into Tuesday. This was unbelievably depressing. I could just imagine my life two years ago, when my dad had driven me up to Maine in that beautiful blue sky, meeting all kinds of friendly people and feeling great about playing basketball. Now I had become Mr. Irrelevant. Nobody cared about me or my abilities. No basketball, no dorm room, and I wasn't walking across campus to meet my friends for lunch. Now I was buying pizza by the slice, so I didn't have to sit alone in the cafeteria like a complete loser. This was a low point for me.

In early September, Mom and Dad laid out the month of October and their surgeries at Winthrop Hospital. That was going to involve me driving my sister to St. Francis Prep before I went to class every day. From St. John's, I would drive to Mineola and spend the evening with my parents in Winthrop. Two years ago, I was traveling all over New England with my teammates and having a blast. Now I was taking one for the family. How could I not do it for my parents, who had been there for me for twenty years? So I made a decision. I needed to get in a gym and play to clear my head. I brought my sneakers with me for the rest of the school year and showed up to Alumni Hall after class to play with the student body. It was the truest form of NYC/schoolyard rules. If you were chosen to play and won, you stayed and played. If you lost, get in your car and go home, because there were twenty-five guys waiting to play. I was able to make a name for myself pretty quickly. I stood out because I had just played two years of college basketball, and my fundamentals were the best in the gym. I rarely lost in these games. The only reasons why I'd leave were that the games got bad or I had to run home. Coach Mahoney was nice enough to make me a practice manager for the 1992-93 season at St. John's, where I was to come to every practice and work out players.

We got to November, and my parents were home feeling better, so I got to see a Division One program practice. First thing that I noticed right away: the size and speed of Division One players is remarkable. You don't get a true feel for it on TV. Junior center Shawnelle Scott was 6'11" and had wide shoulders. Senior David Cain was a 6'0" point guard who could use his deceptive speed to get into the lane. Senior forward Lamont Middleton was strong at 6'6" but played like a seven-footer. Nice group of guys, but the second thing I noticed was that Division One players get treated like celebrities. Head trainer Ron Linfonte was the best in the country. He had two assistant trainers, and four managers rebounding or passing in each drill. Gatorade and water at both ends of the court. Meal money on the road, pregame meals at Dante's on Union Turnpike, ESPN and MSG televising every game, and the St. John's basketball tradition. I found my niche as someone who could make the program better.

After a month had gone by, Coach Mahoney decided to redshirt a freshman from Brentwood named Tom Bayne. Tom was a 6'10" center who came into school thirty-five pounds overweight.

Coach came up to me and said, "Billy, I want you to bring him into the auxiliary gym every day during practice and work him out for two hours. He's at 295, but we need him to be 260."

He was my project, and my chance to show the coaches that I was serious about basketball. I sat him down and told him what we were going to do. I ran him into the ground, we lifted weights six days a week, and he took 500 shots every day. I put him on an eating schedule and wouldn't let him party when we went out as a team. In three months, he was down to 255, and I got into great shape during this time as well. My legs were strong from working at the beach, I played after class every day, and I was in two men's leagues with my high school buddy Gene Devine. St. John's had a great season, getting to the NCAA tourney but losing to Arkansas in the second round. Coach Mahoney was awarded Big East Coach of the Year, and the team had a strong core coming back.

My mom had food on the table almost every night for me. A big upside to living at home. Things were starting to look up. I would visit the guys in Maine when I could, and I spent a lot of time at St. John's and Hofstra bars. As I turned twenty-one in March of 1993, I was having a blast going out with my buddies Pete Hurley, Coz, Gene, and my old friend Mike Gillespie, who transferred home to St. John's from Oneonta. My Rosedale buddies Timmy O'Leary, Walter

Johnson, and Greg Kay asked me to play on their summer softball team in 1993. That created another crew of guys to go out and have fun with. All I did was concentrate on school, hoops, my family, and friends. Always listen to your gut. My decision to transfer home was starting to feel right.

CHAPTER SIXTEEN

THANK YOU, TEDDY ROOSEVELT

TEDDY ROOSEVELT HAS A FAMOUS SPEECH, "The Man in the Arena," that I have lived by since studying it at Westbrook College. This speech was given in 1910 after his two terms as President, and I have applied it to all parts of my life:

"It is not the critic who counts; not the man who points out how the strong man stumbles, or where the doer of deeds could have done them better. The credit belongs to the man who is actually in the arena, whose face is marred by dust and sweat and blood; who strives valiantly; who errs, who comes short again and again, because there is no effort without error and shortcoming; but who does actually strive to do the deeds; who knows great enthusiasms, the great devotions; who spends himself in a worthy cause; who at the best knows in the end the triumph of high achievement, and who at the worst, if he fails, at least fails while daring greatly, so that his place shall never be with those cold and timid souls who neither know victory nor defeat."

President Roosevelt believed that only people in the "arena" could enjoy victory or defeat. The "arena" could be applied to work, sports, family, etc. Taking risks and believing in yourself is the way to leadership. I was not afraid to fail anymore. I'd been cut many times in high school, but Coach Graffam taught me to lead with my heart, just like my father did. I could not be criticized by anyone if I believed in what I was doing. Coach Graffam gave me confidence and self-worth, and taught me how to lead without fear of criticism. He turned me and my teammates from boys into men. These are qualities that I did not possess leaving high school.

Jack Hubbard, the general manager from Sun & Surf, called me in early May of my junior year and wanted me to come in to talk about my assignment for the summer. I drove down to the beach after class at St. John's and we sat down. Usually, locker boys who did a good job would get the responsibility of a cabana court. He had no room for me in the cabanas, so he created a salaried position where I would be the athletic director and play sports with the kids at the club. I would run basketball tournaments, wiffle ball games, and bocce matches. That was okay with me, but I was really looking forward to making cash in the cabanas. I offered to do lockers again, but he said to trust him. I agreed and finished up the school year.

In that first year at St. John's, I sat by myself in the cafeteria a lot. It was good to see Pete Hurley sometimes, but I didn't know a soul. My mom convinced me to get involved in the intramural program for co-ed volleyball and basketball. I ran into an old friend from high school at co-ed volleyball and started playing with a great group of guys and girls. That's when I met the only friend I made at St. John's. Jenn Walsh was a freshman from the Mary Louis Academy who'd gone to St. John's because her mother, Joan, worked in administration. We hit it off and found that we had two classes together, so we'd hang out. Jenn had a brutally honest way of telling it like it is.

We would eat breakfast and lunch together when we could. She would edit my philosophy papers for me, type my English comp essays, and make fun of the girls I liked. There was a very good-looking girl in our theology class, and we would have to walk by her in a big auditorium/classroom to get to our seats.

One day at lunch between classes, Jenn asked me, "Bill, do you think that girl in our theology class is pretty? I think she likes you."

I smiled and said shyly, "Yeah, very nice girl. Maybe I'll ask her on a date after class today. Do you think she'll say yes?"

Jenn responded, "You won't find out unless you ask. See if she wants to go to the movies." I nodded yes with some apprehension, and we got up to go to class.

As we walked into our theology class, I saw the cute girl at the end of our row, so we would have to slide by her on the way to our seats. As we stepped towards her, I smiled at her and she smiled back. I was so excited to talk to her, and then Jenn grabbed my arm and said, "Honey, where are you taking me tonight? I would love to go to a club and go dancing. Will you take me dancing tonight, babe?"

I pulled my arm away and she gave me a cheesy smile. The cute girl turned away, no longer smiling. We walked to our seats, and I yelled at Jenn under my breath, "What the hell are you doing? She was into me, and didn't you say I should ask her out?"

Jenn gave a cute smile of her own and couldn't stop giggling. "You should have seen the look on her face when I spoke. Gotcha!"

Every time that girl looked down the row at me, Jenn put her head on my shoulder and grabbed my arm. And every time Jenn did that, I pulled my arm away and tried to get the cute girl to look at me. But just like high school, I was given the Heisman trophy again. Jenn enjoyed watching me strike out.

In retrospect, thank goodness for Jenn, because I might have gone out of my mind without her. She was a lot of fun and a good friend. It was a big transition, going from knowing everyone on campus at Westbrook to knowing less than ten people at St. John's. We signed up for three classes together in the spring of 1993, and we had a lot of laughs together.

Also during my junior year, I developed a relationship with my Athletic Administration Dean, Bernie Beglane. He was an Associated Press writer for college and pro sports as well as a wonderful professor. For my senior year, he asked me where I wanted to do my internship. I told him WFAN radio in Astoria. He got it done for me, and I was to start in September. There were not many people at St.

John's that I completely trusted, but he was one of them. Dean Beglane became a mentor to me, someone I could trust at St. John's.

A week before Memorial Day weekend, Jack Hubbard of Sun & Surf called me again with a change in assignment. I drove down to Sun & Surf, and Jack asked with a smile on his face, "I would like you to be my assistant in charge of cabana and locker personnel. We'll call the position Cabana Captain."

I said, "I'd love to," right away, but I did ask him about my salary and pay.

Jack replied, "It would be more hours and less money than last year, but a chance for advancement in the future. You're someone I can trust, and you're older, so we made the decision to add you to management."

Most workers would leave two or three weeks before the summer. Since I went to St. John's, I could work until Labor Day and after. There was one thing that concerned me, though—I would now be in charge of my friends like Joe Burns, who got me the job a year before. Joe called my promotion the biggest jump in beach club history. My position was new to the beach club circuit, and it was going to take an open mind and evolving as I went along. My first meeting as Cabana Captain was an introduction to the fifty workers on the Saturday morning of Memorial Day weekend. I had four days to prepare. How would I approach my high school friends? How would I deal with the younger maintenance kids? How would I attack problems? Would the club members approve of me? Why did Jack pick me? I found out in the last two weeks of the summer.

June of 1993 was a lot of fun. We had the Knicks and Bulls in the Eastern Conference Finals; Joe Burns' legendary 21st birthday bash in Rockaway; playing basketball; and spending time in beautiful Long Beach, New York. Chauncey's in Long Beach was a bar and restaurant set on the dunes in the popular west end of the beach. To this day, it's my favorite bar of all time. Working at the beach club in June was slow and gave me a chance to get to know the staff better. I made a point to make a connection with every person that I worked with. I felt a personal connection would go a long way down the road. The members in my old locker section were ecstatic for me. They'd come up with a nickname for me by the 4th of July: "Cabana Bill, king of the cabana boys." It was nice to have responsibility, but with that comes a learning process. I needed to know everything about all fifty workers, learn the names of as many members as I could, and know the inner workings of the club from the restaurant to the lifeguards. That was my job in June. There were two perks to my job: I ate for free, and since I worked late hours, Jack had me come in at 11 a.m. every day. That way, I could go out with my friends until midnight and still get plenty of sleep.

I learned so much about teaching and coaching from my ten years at the beach club. Jack was an excellent mentor and friend. He showed me how to be a leader with compassion and intelligence. Jack didn't have to raise his voice to make a point or correct someone. He criticized with care and then found something good to say to build a person back up. I learned a lot about management from him. When you work day after day with teenagers, you have to know their likes and dislikes. You have to know the music and pop culture they follow. You have to know what motivates them. There's no question that my time at the club helped my teaching and coaching career.

Dealing with day-to-day issues and problem solving was my favorite thing to do. Working with a member when a locker boy lost her beach chair. Helping a maintenance worker get his United States citizenship. Telling a thirteen-year-old boy to go back to his cabana at 11:30 p.m., and the boy telling you to go to hell because his parents are at home and he's here with his older sister. Creating a bond with the staff that work in the bar and kitchen because you have to stay late and close up the club with them three nights a week. My hardest and longest day of the week was on Tuesday, Jack's day off. My friends completely took advantage of me and went on two-hour lunches in Long Beach, where I was put in an awkward position. Being the boss is hard, but I was given a trial by fire in 1993, and I did so well that I was asked back eight more years after that. I spent my twenties working six days a week in the summer at Sun & Surf Beach Club. While a lot of teachers spent time at the beach, I developed into a leader.

In mid-August of 1993, I was driving to the club on a very rare rainy Tuesday for that summer when I got into a car accident with my light blue undercover cop car and totaled it. The entire car crumbled like an accordion when I hit a light pole, and my driver's seat was the only spot saved. The accident was four blocks from my house, and I didn't go to work because my back and neck were injured pretty bad. I'm still dealing with these injuries to this day. I took four days off and came back for the weekend. All summer long, I developed a strong bond with my friend John Lomonaco, who was the personal driver for Mr. Ferguson, the owner of Sun & Surf. John and I spent a lot of time talking about life on those late nights. He was heading back to Marist College, so I took over his driving duties plus mine for the last two weeks of the summer. I was working twelve to sixteen-hour days and making great money.

Mr. Ferguson was a self-made man. He served in Europe as an officer during World War II, then graduated from Yale on the GI Bill and made enough money in the 1950s to buy four beach clubs under the Surf Point Corp. He never married and loved his summers in NY. (He lived in Florida during the winter.) Mr. Ferguson owned a dog who was his companion, and he lived just over the Atlantic Beach Bridge in Lawrence. As I found out from Jack when I started driving him in late August, Mr. Ferguson was dying of cancer and could no longer drive or walk very well. I was to be his right-hand man for two weeks. He told me of liberating France during the war, his stories of leadership in business, and his Yale background. Mr. Ferguson was an interesting man. I spent two weeks driving him, and he told me that I would have to help Jack out in the future. He loved and respected Jack, but he felt I would be a good addition to management.

The last night I drove him back to his house in Lawrence, he asked me to walk him upstairs to his apartment. He wanted to show me pictures of himself in Europe during World War II. At this point, he needed help getting up the stairs due to his illness, and I think he had too much to drink. As we walked into the room, his dog attacked my leg and took a bite out of my right knee. He grabbed her collar and almost fell over. Mr. Ferguson calmed his dog down and gave me a tissue to stop the bleeding. He pulled a couple of books from his shelf and took out pictures for me to look at. One picture was of him on top of a tank in Paris. He gave me his book about the war so I could use it in my classroom one day. I still refer to that book in my US History classes. Mr. Ferguson gave me a very nice tip and wished me luck in school. He was very kind to me.

I work so much better when I know the people leading me have respect for me and appreciate my efforts. Mr. Ferguson and Jack Hubbard were very genuine and professional human beings, and I learned a lot about management from them. Unfortunately, Mr. Ferguson passed away of cancer in early 1994 down in Florida, but I will always remember his kindness.

CHAPTER SEVENTEEN

WHO, ME?

AS THE SUMMER of 1993 ended, Mom was not doing well, but she still seemed to get dinner ready for us every day she could. My dad was feeling better, but once again, I needed a car, as my Dodge Diplomat had been totaled. We bought a 1985 Chrysler LeBaron hatchback for $950.00 from a St. John's student after two weeks of taking the bus and subway. In September of my senior year, I stopped in to see Alex Evans in the St. John's Basketball Office to see how he was doing. I brought up the subject of trying out for the team as a walk-on. A walk-on is defined as a college athlete who was not recruited or does not receive scholarship money to play a sport, and I was completely okay with that. My dream as a 7th-grader in 1985 was to play at St. John's one day. In the fall of 1993, it was highly unlikely, but not impossible.

Alex sat me down and was very honest: "I'll talk to Coach Mahoney, but I'm telling you it's not looking good. We have twelve scholarship players already, but I'll talk to him."

I replied, "Alex, my senior year is going to be very simple. I have a couple of classes and my internship at WFAN. I've already started one day a week, and they know my situation. My goal is to do whatever I can to make our program better."

He thanked me for my help last year as a manager, and I walked out with a mission to get in shape by October 30th. Luckily I had gone through Coach Graffam's boot camp conditioning for two years. The NCAA was trying something new and pushed the season back two weeks from the usual date of October 15th. My lower back was still sore from my late summer car accident, but I was never more ready for the challenge of playing for St. John's University. No guarantee, no promise, but a shot.

This was my plan in late September: map out the next four weeks and create a five-day workout program. In my junior year at St. John's, I had a lot of free time, so I took up weightlifting. That plus beer and pizza got me strong, and I now weighed 220 pounds, up from 190 in my freshman year. I followed my schedule religiously, as well as playing as many pickup games as possible. I ran two miles a day three times a week and lifted weights in between. I was surprised to find how important getting stronger was in basketball. Especially playing inside the paint for my fall league team with Gene Devine.

On Wednesday, October 27th, I was leaving the weight room when I ran into the longtime locker room attendant, Dutch Ouderkirk. He was the eyes and ears of the athletic department, but I didn't know until after he passed away that he was a legendary Suffolk County basketball official, too. He knew the game, and he was the man who got scholarships for managers. He had the inside word on everything. Dutch brought me into the cage where all the athletic equipment was stored and lit up a cigarette. He told me that Coach Mahoney had come to see him about the team. Coach informed him that four players had gotten hurt in their preseason workouts, and he was looking for a couple of walk-ons. Coach Mahoney was asking about my workout habits and how the players got along with me. Dutch gave him nothing but positive reviews. I thanked Dutch, and a feeling of optimism came over me. But again there were no promises.

I went home that day and told Mom and Dad. They were ecstatic and just as optimistic. My father and I went into the backyard to shoot, like we had a thousand times before. He was giving me a pep talk in case Coach Mahoney asked me to try out. Dad had played at the University of Utah in the mid-1950s against Bill Russell and Wilt Chamberlain, and he knew what he was talking about. He sat under the basket rebounding the ball for me and said, "Give 100% effort in every drill and remember all that Coach Graffam taught you. You will be fine." Then he added with a laugh, "You have nothing to lose!" My thoughts raced that night.

The next day, I was doing my two-mile run in the rectangular hallway basement of Alumni Hall when Alex Evans and Coach Mahoney walked towards me. Alex waved me over to where they were standing outside the locker room. This was nerve-wracking, to say the least, but Alex calmed me down by starting off with his catch-phrase and smile, "There he is...LEGEND!"

I replied with a smile, "Hi, Coach. Hi Alex."

Coach Mahoney said with a smile, "Hey, Billy, we have some lingering injuries with the team right now that might last a month or so. We need a couple of bodies to help us in practice. Report to the team practice Saturday morning at 9:00 a.m. See Dutch for a practice uniform. Let's see how you do Saturday."

I was beyond thrilled! My dream had come true. My response was very simple. "Thank you for this opportunity, Coach. I won't let you down." We shook hands and they walked into the locker room together. I sprinted with a smile and met with Dutch, who was smiling more than I was. He had my practice gear in a bag waiting for me with the number 31. I opened it up and found a practice jersey, practice shorts, red and blue spandex, a gray t-shirt, a white t-shirt, and an extra large blue sweatshirt that said ST. JOHN'S BASKET-BALL #31. I was in shock and disbelief, and so happy I couldn't believe it. Dutch asked me to tell Bradley Small to come see him if I ran into him. Bradley was a quick guard who played pickup with me every day, and we got along well.

I drove home, and Mom was so happy for me that she made my favorite meal, chicken cutlets and mashed potatoes. My first reaction was to call my friends to inform them of my good news, but I didn't want to jinx it. My dad got home, and we ate with smiles on our faces. It was definitely a good day. When Greg and Timmy called me to go out drinking, I told them that I was going to stay in and watch *Seinfeld* with my parents. They understood, and I slept well that night.

My internship in the fall was on Fridays at WFAN from 10 in the morning to 2 in the afternoon. I would walk up the stairs to the Promotions and Marketing department, where I would work with Tammy Restuccia and Mark Finkelstein. Very good people who were helpful to me. Their boss was the great marketing guru Harry Spero, who created the legendary 1980s advertisement for Crazy Eddie electronics: "These prices are INSANE." Harry was a funny guy who asked me to do errands into NYC for him. I loved taking the train into Manhattan as a delivery boy, dropping off important documents, picking up his dry cleaning, etc. I felt comfortable at WFAN, but the one thing you didn't do was bother the talent. I picked up on that quickly. Don't talk to Imus, and leave Mike & the Mad Dog alone. Although one fun part of my job was to go to WFAN Promotions parties in various places around the metro area. That's where I got to meet people like Mike Breen, Bernard McGuirk, Ian Eagle, and plenty others. It was a fun internship.

On Friday, October 29th, I couldn't think about anything else but Saturday morning. I took the train to Kaufman Astoria Studios, and I was going to drive home with Dad on his way home from Long Island City. He picked me up that afternoon in Astoria, and we had a great talk on the way home. Mom wasn't feeling great, so Dad and I had leftover chicken cutlets on Italian bread. He made some lumpy mashed potatoes for us, and we sat and watched TV after dinner. I went to bed early, because I wanted to be at St. John's by 8:00 a.m. to warm up and shoot around early. My dad wished me good luck and gave me a big hug good night. Mom got up out of bed to see me before

I went upstairs. She didn't feel good on certain days. It depended on her blood pressure and vertigo. I don't know how she moved as well as she did, but her will was strong and her faith was even stronger.

Saturday morning came, and I was dressed in my practice uniform and sweatshirt on that beautiful day. I was in the gym at 8:00 a.m. shooting around, all by myself. I had been in Alumni Hall before, but never in a practice uniform. This was an exhilarating moment, shooting around by myself like Chris Mullin had done ten years before. And then two people appeared out of the locker room doors downstairs at Alumni Hall, a young woman and a little boy who was probably ten years old. The woman was professionally dressed, but the boy looked somewhat disheveled. His clothes were tattered, but he had a smile on his face. They watched me shoot for a couple of minutes, and then I asked the little boy if he wanted to shoot. The woman was so excited that I'd asked—she looked to be his mentor. The little boy put his head down. He came over and I introduced myself. His name was Jon, and I finally coaxed him into joining me. I worked with him for ten minutes or so. I showed him how to shoot a basketball the way my father had taught me, and after some difficulties, he hit some shots and started to smile. His mentor Jackie was so thrilled. When she saw our training staff enter the other side of the gym, she whispered to Jon and made him shake my hand before they left. "Good luck with the season," she said.

As they walked out, my good friend from sports management class, Derek Brown, walked in to stretch with our trainer Ron Linfonte. Derek was the most athletic guard on the team and looked at me in shock, as he didn't know I was working out today. He smiled and told me to do my thing.

As the players came in the door, some reacted to me being in practice gear and some didn't. Carl Beckett immediately came up to me and shook my hand. Carl was an amazing person and athlete from Christ the King HS in Queens. He was a year older than me and played on one of the best high school teams I've ever seen; the 1988-89 Royals had Carl (SJU), Khalid Reeves (Arizona) who eventually had a solid NBA career, Derrick Phelps (UNC) who was the starting point guard on the 1993 National Championship Tar Heel team, Jamal Faulkner (Arizona State), and Sherwin Content (Fordham). That's not including the plethora of bench players who were tough and reliable. Carl was a great guy and a wonderful teammate. All we did was talk NYC hoops and argue over who was better: Molloy or Christ the King. Shawnelle Scott was another senior who I knew from the Catholic League, who had knocked out Molloy two years in a row for All Hallows. He was a larger-than-life big man who would be our star that year.

Bradley Small, the other walk-on, found me immediately, and we bonded for a couple of minutes before the coaching staff entered. He had a similar upbringing to mine. Bradley grew up close by me in Jamaica, Queens, and had a love for baseball. He and I were the same age, and he was cut all four years from the basketball team at August Martin High School. Bradley was a quick 5'9" point guard who could shoot really well. He blossomed late in life, like myself, and walked on the basketball team at Syracuse University in his freshman year. We knew each other from Queens playgrounds and local men's leagues.

Bradley and I were going to look out for each other and do the best we could. There were only eight players dressed and four scholarship guys on the sideline getting treatment for leg injuries. It was strange, because at Westbrook, we never had anyone banged up, and if we did, we would never admit it. The coaching staff walked in five minutes before 9:00: head coach Brian Mahoney, longtime assistants Ron Rutledge and Al LoBalbo, and new assistant coach George Felton from South Carolina. They got everyone in the middle and explained practice, as well introducing myself and Bradley as practice players. Practice would go from 9:00 a.m. until noon, and Coach Mahoney brought the walk-ons to the side and explained that we had to go into the auxiliary gym at noon with Coach Felton for the official walk-on tryout for two hours with the student body. I didn't know about an extra workout, but I was in great shape, so I would "get it done." That's what Coach Graffam would say.

Practice started with energy and enthusiasm, and for about forty minutes we ran full court with finishing drills. I watched and learned quickly, as did Bradley. What I didn't know was that Bradley had walked on at Syracuse as a freshman three years earlier. I was pretty impressed, but he was in the same boat as me. We both came home to St. John's under similar circumstances and wanted to keep playing. Then Coach LoBalbo took over with his defensive scheme. As I learned quickly, it was extremely similar to the Westbrook system. "BALL-U-MAN," he screamed over and over again, and I knew what he meant. In his defensive system, if you are not guarding the man with the ball, that player will stand on the help-side line and point to the ball and his man. It's the same system we were taught by Coach Graffam. One of the returning players wasn't picking it up, so he put me in, and I started to point to the BALL and my MAN. He was amazed that I knew his system, and that went a long way in that first practice. We got halfway done, and Coach Rutledge came up to us and said we were really doing great. He noted that we were needed to compete in drills, and our energy was exceptional. Coach Rutledge was a positive influence on our team.

The last hour or so was learning the half court offense, something I hadn't done since Molloy; at Westbrook, we ran a fast-paced/high-powered offense. Coach Mahoney had a very specific set of plays designed for Shawnelle Scott and a new JUCO transfer, James Scott. James was an All-American junior college player who could handle the ball and score from anywhere. Playing the point was not the best place for him, and this did not please Mo Brown. Mo was a sophomore point guard from Grady High School in Brooklyn who was the public school player of the year in 1992. Mo was a great guy who could lead a team on and off the court. I loved the way he got everyone the ball. Mo was a New York City point guard through and through. This is where myself and Bradley would sit on the side and take it in. We knew our role on day one. When we were doing drills, we were involved. Defense with Coach LoBalbo, we were definitely in. Shooting stations, we had our own basket. But when the coaches ran the plays for the starters, we would take a spot to the side. As practice ended, we broke down in the middle, and I really felt I'd done a great job, as I'd done at Molloy in practices my senior year, as well as at Westbrook.

The administrative assistant, Alex Evans, couldn't be at practice, but he was waiting at the door for all the players as they exited. He walked with myself and Bradley to get a drink on the way to the other gym. He warned us that Coach Felton was running the practice and he was tough. Most people would have sighed, but I was fired up. I welcomed it because I was ready and in shape. I had a great opportunity in front of me that I had worked so hard for, and no one was going to take it from me. But that walk-on tryout really was tough. There were about twelve players trying to make the team with myself and Bradley. I knew most of the players from running fullcourt games after school. Without question, I had the most college experience and was the most fundamentally sound player, but Coach Felton was running us into the ground. He had us sprinting fullcourt with fast break drills, and working halfcourt in one-on one competition. My lower back was starting to act up, but I wouldn't let anyone know it. After the workout, he thanked everyone for coming down and said they would be in touch. Coach Felton tapped myself and Bradley on the shoulder and asked us to meet him in the locker room. We got inside, but the team had left hours ago. He said to find our lockers and hit the showers. The practice schedule was on the wall. He left us, and Bradley and I danced without any music and jumped in the air. My locker was in between Carl Beckett and freshman star Roshown McLeod from St. Anthony in New Jersey. I showered and got home as quick as I could.

I walked into an empty house and sat in the backyard with delight. I wouldn't take off my St. John's basketball sweatshirt—there was no way it was coming off. I stayed in again, to relax on a Saturday night, for the first time in three years, and prepared for the Sunday afternoon practice. This one was more intense and chock-full of details. I had a lot to learn, but another player got hurt. This was bad. Nine healthy bodies in practice was not a good sign, because our first game was in two weeks. Every day was exciting nonetheless, and I was now a member of the practice squad.

Coach Mahoney grabbed us after practice and said we were doing a good job, that our hard work was really helping the team. He also noted that the other players liked us and our work habits. That was so nice to hear after day two. But the look on Coach Mahoney's face changed as we walked toward the trainer's room to talk to Ron Linfonte. Our team was banged up.

Days later, Alex Evans showed me a letter addressed to Coach Mahoney about me. It explained how I had helped a young man on Saturday morning, and how I would make a wonderful coach one day. How prophetic was Jackie, as I was thinking about education and coaching for my future. And I think her letter might have solidified my role on the St. John's basketball team.

My good friend Gene Devine had left SJU before his senior year to join the NYPD, and he called me to see how it was going. We agreed to meet at J.P.O.D.'s on Wednesday night to have some beers. That was the hot night at SJU for drinking and dancing. We had a blast, but Gene was a little upset because we had talked about trying out together senior year. He couldn't pass up the NYPD. Gene was a great shooter and a basketball lifer like myself.

As the week progressed, some guys came back healthy and some got hurt again. I think they attributed this outbreak of injuries to the preseason conditioning program. Bradley and I were fine because we weren't involved. A week later, the annual Red/White scrimmage was cancelled because we only had ten bodies. That would risk injury, and meant I would have to play the entire game. No one was going to pay to see me shoot. The walk-ons are expected to know their role: helping in practice, and that's it.

As we got closer to our first game on November 16th, Coach Mahoney really appreciated our work ethic and unselfish play in practice. He made a decision to allow Bradley and myself to dress for home games only, though we were not to travel. He told us one day before the first home game. I was ecstatic, and didn't have time to call my friends to let them know that I was warming up with the team and sitting on the bench. My parents were so proud when I told them the good news, especially Dad. He was the driving force behind not letting me quit, and implored me to follow my dream. This dream came true all because I was in the right place at the right time, and I took advantage of my opportunity. My father had been correct.

Due to the injuries and late start by the NCAA, we lost our first home game to Towson State. This was a shock to the basketball world. We were slated to come in the top four of the Big East, along with Boston College, UConn, and Syracuse. It was a part of the preseason NIT, and a chance to play at Madison Square Garden before Thanksgiving. We had problems at the point guard position. It was going to be hard to replace a solid floor general in David Cain. Also, we had a problem with leadership. As good as our older players were, they could not lead like David. He, along with power forward Lamont Middleton, was the glue that held the team together in the 1992-93 season. Last year's team had made it to the second round of the NCAA tournament because David and Lamont were New York City street tough. They refused to lose, and David was the point guard who players wanted to follow. Very similar to Teddy Quinn up at Westbrook. As a practice manager, I realized right away that we had more leadership up at Westbrook than St. John's did.

Another issue was all twelve scholarship players thought they should be on the court over the next guy. Roles were not well-defined, and early on, I don't think any one player (with the exception of Shawnelle at center) set himself apart enough that they could not be taken out of the lineup. After the Towson loss, our next two weeks of practices were tough and competitive. Due to this loss, we did not have another game until November 30th with Columbia. There would be no Madison Square Garden the nights before and after

Thanksgiving. That was a bummer, but I was still going to suit up against Columbia.

Those two weeks allowed us to get healthy. Coach Mahoney announced an open tryout at the guard and forward positions, so players who were banged up got healthy all of a sudden. Suddenly everyone started to compete at a high level. Sophomore power forward Charlie Mineland and point guard Maurice Brown were playing well. Junior Derek Brown looked good at shooting guard. James Scott was our small forward, and Shawnelle Scott at the center position rounded out our best starting lineup going into the early season. We had a strong bench, of Seniors Carl Beckett and Lee Green, Sophomores Fred Lyson and Rowan Barrett, and Freshman Roshown McLeod. There was optimism for our team. That meant less reps in practice for me and Bradley, but that was good for the team all in all. It was great to see our team get better by the day, and my goal was to do anything possible to make the Redmen great.

The November 30th Columbia game was here, and for the last week and a half, my buddies were calling to see if I was dressing for the game. My longtime friend Walter Johnson from Rosedale was in St. John's Law School, and we played summer softball together. He and our other softball teammates, Gerry Polizzi and Ernie Hambrock, had season tickets for all the home games. They were ready to cheer on the Redmen, and they couldn't believe someone who hadn't played one minute of high school basketball was now warming up in uniform for St. John's.

Four hours before every game at St. John's, there was a team dinner at Dante's, an Italian restaurant on Union Turnpike. This food was outstanding, and we had a choice of chicken, fish, or steak— and, of course, pasta. We would eat as a team, walk back to campus, go to the locker room, and get dressed for the game. I don't remember the first game with Towson St. because it was a blur, but I remember the Columbia game well. For some reason, I felt like we had come together as a team from that first loss, and the determination on our faces was noticeable.

We would go out, stretch as a team, and then shoot around until there was thirty-five minutes before game time. That's when we would go back to the locker room and get matchups and strategy from Coach Mahoney and the coaching staff. Coach Mahoney always wrote detailed scouting reports that I will never forget. Height, weight, class, strengths, weaknesses, etc. I use that today with my coaching for games. He also believed in showing film of the other team, as well as ours. Sometimes he would show it the day before or pregame.

On this night, there was no film, no rah rah speeches; only a team that wanted to win and gain back the good graces of the Alumni Hall fanbase. If you know anything about St. John's fans, you know they are without a doubt the most faithful and dedicated sports fans in college basketball. People have passed down their season tickets from generation to generation. But there was one fan I looked for immediately: my father. He could not get to the first game because Mom was sick, but he wasn't going to miss this one. I was waiting excitedly to come out the Alumni Hall doors, warm up with the team, and wave to him. He was going to sit with my friends Timmy and Greg from Rosedale, and one of my friends from Molloy, Mike Gillespie, who had transferred into St. John's like I did. As the team got together one last time before the doors opened, we prayed in a circle and screamed, "WE ARE...ST. JOHN'S!"

I'm not sure I've been ever this excited and nervous all at once, before or since, because my friends and Dad were waiting to see me and I didn't want to let them down. These were the people who'd supported me when I was ready to give up. As a walk-on, my role during a game was to support and clap for my teammates. Win or lose, I was going to cheer like a fan. I had the best seat in the house, and if I wasn't on the team, I would have been in the crowd cheering anyway.

We ran out in height order, with our senior captains Shawnelle Scott and Carl Beckett in the rear. Our team would run from our bench side to the other basket and perform a line of throwing the ball off the backboard, with the last player finishing the layup. Then we would break up into layup lines. Angelo and my friends were standing and calling out my name. It was exhilarating. I was flying instead of running and jumping. I couldn't stop sweating or smiling. No one told me what to do on the warm up, so I just followed everyone else. I did something I learned later wasn't allowed, but I didn't care; I waved to Dad. I couldn't control myself. He was always there for me in baseball and basketball, driving me from game to game, picking me up late at night, working seven days a week for years. How could I not wave and show respect to my hero?

Fifteen seconds later, Coach LoBalbo grabbed me to the side and screamed, "Billy, I don't give a shit if the President of the United States is waving to you! Act like a professional. We're here to get focused and win."

I replied, "Yes, Coach." I didn't want to piss him off—he was a great coach and I actually understood his defensive system.

As the warmup time wound down to zero, I got those butterflies in my stomach, even though I had no chance of playing. The buzzer sounded, and the normal pregame starting lineups were to be announced. I did catch Walter, Gerry, and Ernie yelling to me from the stands. The student section was directly across our bench, so that was going to be fun to watch. I also noticed that the MSG Network would be carrying our games this year. Bruce Beck and Bucky Waters were the announcers. The St. John's Alumni Hall public announcer was the legendary Bob Sheppard. He was the voice of the Yankees and Giants, and a professor of public speaking at St. John's. Everything was perfect. Chris Mullin, Mark Jackson, Walter Berry, Bill Wennington, and Malik Sealy had all played on this court, and now I was a part of this legendary program.

As I sat on the end of the bench where the walk-ons sit, next to me was another wonderful person: Dr. Irving Glick, the team orthopedist. He came to every home game with us that year. What a nice man. He congratulated me on making the team, and had nothing but nice things to say about everyone. Doc Glick mentioned that the coaches were happy with my work ethic, and that I deserved to be on the bench in uniform. He made me smile.

We got out to an early lead, as Shawnelle, Charles Mineland, and James Scott were able to score at will against the overmatched Columbia Lions. We went into the locker room with a nice lead at halftime. Our team was on a mission to demoralize and finish off our opponent. As we came out of the locker room for the second half, I noticed the St. John's student section, where Gerry was holding a piece of paper with "BILL" written in bold lettering. He was holding it up in the air and trying to get his grad school buddies to join him in chanting my name. Walter and Ernie got their law school pals to do the same. I had a huge smile on my face, but we had a job to do. The second half started the same way it finished. We had complete control. But something was building with five minutes left. A chant from the student section: "WE WANT BILL! WE WANT BILL! WE WANT BILL!" led by my friends. Nobody in the stands knew who I was, because Bradley and I were added so late to the team that we weren't in the game program or roster. The team picture had been taken before the season.

At the four-minute TV timeout, Carl Beckett came down to speak to me and said, "Those must be your weirdo Molloy friends. Get ready, they might be shaming Mahoney into putting you in."

That's when I almost passed out on the court. I never thought in a million years that I would be playing tonight. My uniform was funny because my last name barely fit on the back of my jersey. It was a semi-circle around the number 31. There were a couple of other people around the gym who recognized me, so they joined into the chant for my entry into the game. With three minutes left, the chant got louder as we opened up the game to thirty points. Bradley and I made a pact: we would look for each other on the court so we could get shots up and potentially score. At the 2:20 mark, we were sitting at the end of the bench and facing forward, cheering on our team-mates, when Coach Mahoney walked down towards us.

Coach looked at me and said, "Billy, who are those people chanting your name?"

I replied, "My summer softball team from Rosedale."

He said, "Billy, Bradley, go in for Mo and Charlie."

Oh my goodness, what do I do? I followed Bradley as we took off our shooting shirts, walking excitedly toward midcourt, and the crowd went wild. We walked quickly to the scorer's table, and the Hall of Fame announcer Bob Sheppard looked at Bradley and said, "What's your name?" in his majestic voice.

"Bradley Small, sir," he replied.

Sheppard then looked in my direction and said, "Son, what's your name?" I smiled because I was talking to the great Bob Sheppard and said, as loud as I could, "Billy Mitaritonna."

With a puzzled look, he said, "Say that again, young man," as the horn sounded at the 1:59 mark and we started to walk onto the court. I couldn't believe I was walking in to play for St. John's nine years after I'd fallen in love with this storied program. Bradley pointed to Mo Brown and shook his hand, as I pointed to Charlie to do the same. The St. John's crowd who stayed for the blowout win got louder than they had at any time all night.

Bob Sheppard then announced our entry into the game with no mention of our names on the roster. "Now entering the game, number eleven, Bradley Small, and number thirty-one, Billy...number thirty-one..."

He couldn't say my last name, which was absolutely hysterical. He was a professor of public speaking and he couldn't get it right. The greatest sports announcer in New York sports history couldn't pronounce my last name.

I ran in and instantly found a man to cover. It was a buddy of mine from the Rockaway summer league, Jimmy Tubridy. He laughed as he saw me come towards him. I think he was laughing at my uniform, which was as tight as anything I've ever worn. My last name was a semi-circle around the number 31. This was going to be fun.

The first possession was Columbia ball, and they made a pass towards the basket that no one touched. I thought it was our ball, but the officials called same way. Columbia then threw a pass that I deflected and tipped to Lee Green. He took it the length of the court for a layup but got fouled. As he went to the line to shoot two free throws, Shawnelle was yelling at him to give me and Bradley the ball. Lee was mad that he hadn't played a lot in this game after not playing well against Towson. Understandable, but I didn't care. Some time went by as I went back and forth down the court, not touching the ball, but Bradley put up a three-pointer and scored. I was so happy for him.

Columbia came down and missed, and we had the ball. Roshown McLeod was fouled shooting, and Bradley came up to me and said, "Bill, I got you next. Be ready." He pounded his fist into my shoulder to encourage me. On the next possession, Columbia scored with about thirty seconds left, and I broke out down the right sideline, like I had so many times in the St. Francis de Sales summer league and for Westbrook College. I was trained to run the break a certain way, with my lead hand up to receive the ball. Bradley got the ball up the court to me so quick, and I caught it right in front of our bench. I could hear Shawnelle Scott and Derek Brown yell, "Shoot it!"

I took one dribble to gather my feet and let it fly. In the back of my mind, I wanted to hit rim and not throw up an airball, so I shot it long off the back rim. The crowd sighed in unison, "Ohhhhhhhhh." That was really nice to hear. My workout buddy from the year before, Tom Bayne, got the rebound and finished it. Now there were only twenty seconds left, and Columbia took about twelve seconds to score. We let them because we would have another chance to get a shot up. With six seconds left after the made basket, Bradley threw the ball to me from out of bounds as I raced towards half court. With two seconds left, I chucked up a halfcourt shot that went just wide of the rim, and the bench and remaining crowd sighed again. But it didn't matter that I didn't score. I played two minutes on TV for St. John's! My father and friends got me into the game and we won.

What a special night. One that will go down in my memory forever. We shook hands with Columbia and ran into the locker room. Coach Mahoney congratulated us on such a team performance, and thanked Shawnelle for his leadership and solid game. We had our first Big East game at Madison Square Garden coming up, so we were going to be off tomorrow.

After the game, news reporters came into the locker room and interviewed Shawnelle and James Scott. Coach gave them some sound bites, and each player went into the shower. These were good times to bring recruits into the locker room to speak with the players. A tall young man from Long Island entered the room: Zendon Hamilton, who was 6'11" and smiling from ear to ear about the possibility of playing for the Redmen. I was sitting with Bradley at my locker when Coach Mahoney and Coach Rutledge came up to me.

Coach Mahoney asked me a question. "Billy, who are those guys in the bleachers?" I smiled and responded, "They are my friends from my summer softball team from Rosedale, who go to law school here. They have season tickets."

He said, "They got you into the game, you better thank them," gave us a high five, and walked out.

After a game at St. John's, friends and family can meet the players upstairs in the lobby. As I came up the stairs, my dad and friends were standing together. I gave each one of them a bro hug and thanked each one for getting me into the game. We had a lot of laughs and spoke for ten minutes. Dad decided to go home because it was getting late, and my friends wanted to bring me out for a beer. I had to go out, but I promised Dad I would check in with Mom before I went to bed to tell her about the experience. After a couple of hours at J.P.O.D.'s, hanging with my friends, I decided to call it a night and get home. Mom was up waiting for me, with the VCR tape all set to go. She'd taped the game for me. How lucky was I for my mom to do this for me? We watched the last two minutes and laughed hysterically. The announcer, Bruce Beck, was very nice to the two walk-ons. He mentioned our previous colleges and said our names right. I went to bed with a big smile on my face; I couldn't wait for school the next day.

When I got to Dean Beglane's athletic administration class the next day, he said something very funny.

"Hey, Billy," he said. "I saw a movie recently with my wife. The name of the movie is *Rudy*. Ha ha—you're the Rudy of St. John's basketball!" He was referring to the story of a young man who beats the odds to play for the Notre Dame Fighting Irish football team. I hadn't seen it, but our class laughed anyway.

I didn't have a lot of friends in Marillac Hall at St. John's, but I was going to be in full Redmen basketball sweats. Here's the thing about a commuter school: nobody cares about you being on the basketball team, because a lot of students don't go to games. My good friend Jenn Walsh said I better not get a big head or she wouldn't be my friend anymore. She had no problem telling me that no one cared if I scored thirty points or none. Jenn had a great way of bringing me down to earth. The St. John's fanbase were people from the 1960s-1980s, "the Glory Years." Those were the Redmen teams that made the school so popular. The athletes on campus all supported each other, which was great, but most of the 19,500 students were there to drive to school, get an education, and go home. Nobody cared that I got two minutes of playing time, nobody cared that I was on TV the night before, and with the exception of my family and friends, nobody cared that I was mentioned in two newspaper articles. It was my close family and friends that cared about me. My Uncle Richie in New Jersey taped every game we had on TV and made a collection for me. My Uncle Johnny in Georgia cut out the *New York Times* article that read "Walk-ons thrill in St. John's win over Columbia." Mike Gillespie handed me the *New York Daily News* article from the Marillac Hall cafeteria, which mentioned that I got playing time. That was really nice of them, to do that for me. I was excited to be a part of the St. John's basketball program.

CHAPTER EIGHTEEN

THE NEXT COUPLE of days at practice were fun. Everyone felt better to have gotten in the win column, but there were some selfish attitudes due to a lack of playing time. That does happen early in the season to a lot of teams. Up next was Seton Hall at the Garden, and I couldn't wait to get there. Actually, getting playing time at Madison Square Garden was beyond my wildest dreams. As we pulled up to 33rd Street, between 7th and 8th Avenue, the bus stopped next to the side entrance to the World's Most Famous Arena. As we walked off the bus into the cold, early December air, we could smell that distinctive New York City odor. Filled with the coal bricks from hot dog stands and the subway stacks, that smell can be tough to handle. It gives New York that toughness that every basketball player needs. Every kid from the five boroughs wants to play at Madison Square Garden. And now I had the chance to shoot around where the New York Knicks played, in a year when they had a chance to win it all. Bradley and I were dressed to play on the bus, so we could get out to the Garden floor and shoot as quickly as possible.

Teams playing at the Garden enter through a secret side door and walk downstairs to the locker room level. Pictures of famous athletes and performers line the walls as you enter the arena. I was in complete awe of the entire building. We sat at our lockers, I put my bag away, and Bradley and I ran out to the court. The arena was empty, with the exception of a few people at the scorer's table. We were so early that the gigantic Jumbotron that hovered over center court was actually on the court. Midcourt was engulfed by this massive scoreboard. Bradley and I started warming up and immediately shooting threes. It was exhilarating. Our team started to come outside to shoot, and I went right into my role as rebounder for the shooting guards, Derek Brown and Fred Lyson. At other times, I would do post passing and big man moves with Shawnelle and Charlie. It was fun to help my teammates get better and prepared for the game. We went back into the locker room with forty-five minutes before game time, and people were starting to find their seats.

This was an important game, both for us and Seton Hall. It was the first Big East game, and both teams wanted to get off to a fast start in the conference. Coach had a meticulous game plan ready for us. He was ready, our team was ready, and we were playing at Madison Square Garden. I liked our chances. We played well that night and the crowd was behind us. I grabbed a towel at the end of the bench and started spinning it during timeouts and big plays for us. (Just like M.L. Carr for the Boston Celtics in the 1980s.) Our starting five played well, and Shawnelle was our anchor. We ended up winning, and what a thrill to play at the Garden. There was some mumbling by some of the bench players in the locker room about playing time, and I didn't like it. In fact, it drove me crazy. But there was no way I was going to say anything because I was new and a walk-on, so I let the veteran players handle it. We got back on the bus and headed home. We were given sandwiches and drinks for the ride—it was really nice how I was treated, even though I didn't have a scholarship.

Our next game was three days later at Alumni Hall against Pittsburgh, and that didn't go well. We didn't play together as a team, and the playing time issue came up again after the loss. At the time, I didn't understand why players complained about minutes. These twelve players were getting a full ride, monthly stipends to live off campus, free meals, all the gear and sneakers they wanted, and the notoriety and alumni connections that come with playing for St. John's. I always looked at the big picture competitively. I wanted to win, and I would do anything to help, but I might have been one of the few who thought about that. When roles are not well established, players do not know how to help the team win. I learned a lot about roles and used this experience later in my high school coaching career.

Coach Mahoney took us to practice at SUNY-Purchase one day, and none of the players knew why. Why would we travel upstate to practice? I called Joe Burns before we left and told him about traveling up to Purchase. Joe was in the middle of his senior year, playing basketball at Manhattanville College in Purchase. He said he would sneak in to see us practice. As we pulled up, we saw Knicks logos and really expensive cars in the parking lot. When we walked in, the 1993-94 New York Knicks were practicing. Here I am, in my St. John's gear with my teammates, and Patrick Ewing, Charles Oakley, John Starks, and Anthony Mason were shooting free throws downstairs. Our coaches walked downstairs to say hello, and our team was to watch practice upstairs with some of the New York sports media. Standing on the other side of the court was Coach Curran from Molloy. He walked over to the Knicks coaches, along with the St. John's coaches, standing in a circle talking basketball. We were waved down by our coaching staff to say hello to the Knicks players before our practice. This was unbelievable, a chance to meet the Knicks and talk to Coach Curran.

Every Knick stayed to talk to us but Patrick Ewing, who played for Georgetown and hated St. John's. I went right up to Oakley and Mason, my two favorite players. I told Mason I was from Rosedale, and he calmly said, "Cool, man, cool." He asked if I went to Springfield Gardens High School, but I said no. I told them both how much I modeled my game on theirs, though I was of course six inches shorter. They smiled and told us, "Good luck this season!" I was in basketball heaven.

Coach Mahoney then waved me over to the circle of coaches to see Coach Curran. He was old friends with our assistant coach, George Felton. Coach Curran said, "How're you doing, Billy? How's it going? Are you the manager?" He asked me in front of Brian Mahoney, Ron Rutledge, Pat Riley, George Felton, Jeff Van Gundy, and Al LoBalbo. A lot of things entered my mind as he asked me that question. I looked at everyone and responded very politely, "Good to see you, Coach. Actually, I made the team as a walk-on."

You have to know how Coach Curran would respond sometimes —he had a very funny laugh, and it's hard to describe. "HUH HUH HUH! Good for you, Billy!" All of the coaches loved and respected Coach Curran, so they laughed too. I shook Pat Riley and Jeff Van Gundy's hands and thanked them for having us there to practice. Coach Curran had been right about me when I was in high school. I wasn't that good at age seventeen, and he was right about me being more valuable to him as a manager. But at the same time, he could have added myself, Joe Burns, Joe Grimpel, and Mark Turner. We were all good enough to practice against the team and maybe play a little during our senior season. Coach Curran took eleven players on the roster our senior year. As a high school coach today, I always add two to three extra players to the end of the roster who know their role and help us in practice. It has always been a positive experience for these kids, and I still keep in touch with those players today. I call them my "walk-ons."

The Knicks left, and we started practice. Coach Rutledge came up to me and asked if I knew that person up top in the viewing area, and I said, "Yes, Coach, that's my best friend Joe Burns. He plays at Manhattanville College. He wanted to see our practice."

He came downstairs and sat with Coach Curran. Joe had been recommended by Coach Curran to play at Manhattanville, even though he didn't play varsity at Molloy either. Coach Curran did that for a lot of players at Molloy, and kids from other schools as well. He did have a kind heart, despite his gruff exterior.

There are not many practices in college that I remember, but I absolutely remember this one. I wanted to show Coach Curran that I had improved and deserved to be a part of the St. John's basketball program. There were two plays that stood out for me. Twelve players were practicing today, and Sergio Luyk and Tom Bayne were sitting out, so Bradley and I were needed. Coach LoBalbo was running the defensive shell drill and I was on defense. The ball was rotated by the offense from one side to the other in the drill, and the defense had to help, slide, and recover. I stepped in and took a charge on Fred Lyson as he went to the basket. He wasn't a strong guy, but he was 6'7". I took it square in the chest, and the team started clapping while I was on the floor. Carl Beckett sprinted over and picked me up.

My four-man team left the floor, and Coach Mahoney came up to me and said, "Nice job, Billy, but let's not get the scholarship guys hurt." I looked at him and said, "Yes, Coach," and I could hear Coach Graffam cringing up in Maine. At Westbrook, we would practice taking charges once a week. But this was a Division One Big East program, with a lot of time and resources invested. It was his team, so I understood.

Later in that practice, we were running a fast break drill, and I had the ball out on the left wing sprinting towards the basket. James Scott was an athletic swingman coming at me full speed from midcourt. I took two power dribbles down the lane to the left of the basket, jump stopped off two feet, shot faked, and watched James jump through the roof. As he came down, I put the ball in off the glass, nice and soft. The coaches stopped practice to make a point of my nice play. Coach Rutledge always tapped me on the back when I did something good. He was a positive force in our program and a wonderful recruiter. I looked over to Joe Burns, who was smiling. This day was as good as it got for me all season. Coach Curran left, and Joe followed him close after. As we got on the bus to go home, Wayne Coffey, an excellent sportswriter from the *Daily News*, approached myself and Bradley about an article he was writing about walk-ons for next Sunday. He would be in touch about when he would talk to us at practice next week. This day could not have gone better!

As we prepared for the annual Lapchick Tournament on the weekend of December 11th, Wayne Coffey came into practice on the Thursday before, with a photographer as advertised. He did a great job of asking questions about my past: being a St. John's fan since 1985, my father's background in basketball, and my journey from not playing one minute of high school basketball to the Big East. He interviewed us and other walk-ons from Syracuse and Seton Hall, but he brought myself and Brad outside to the gates at St. John's for photos. They also took pictures of us sitting on the bench at Saturday's game against Colgate in the first round of the Lapchick Tournament. I couldn't believe the week I was having. Two months ago, I was taking the Q111 Jamaica bus to school and playing in men's league games, and now I was playing at Madison Square Garden, wearing a St. John's uniform!

Saturday morning came, and I got there early to watch my other best friend from Molloy, Pat Cosgrove, who was playing for Hofstra against Yale in the first game of our tournament. He looked great, but they were losing with ten minutes left in the game. We had to go inside to get dressed, and as I walked past the Colgate players, I saw my social studies teacher and the man who cut me from the JV basketball team at Molloy, Coach Rich Sutter. He was a great guy, and left Molloy after three years to become a college assistant at Colgate. Coach Curran made a call and got him the job. I yelled to him from down the hall, "Coach Sutter! How are you doing?"

He seemed surprised to see me walking with the team into our locker room. "Billy Mitaritonna. Great to see you...what are you doing here?" I couldn't believe for the second time in a week I was going to run into a coach who'd cut me in high school. But I felt I deserved to make the JV in my sophomore year.

"I'm on the team here at St. John's," I said. "Some of your favorite players are here today. Pat Cosgrove plays for Hofstra, and Jeff Wilkins from Molloy is sitting with my dad at the game as well."

He smiled and said, "Wow. Awesome, let's talk after the game. Good luck."

As we finished reading the scouting report in the St. John's home locker room, the crowd erupted, and Coach Rutledge walked in close after. "Hey, Bill, your boy just hit a game-winning shot for Hofstra."

Good for Pat, he deserved it. His entire family was here, sitting with my family. Also my good friend from Molloy, John Mavroukas, was playing with Pat as well, so there was a big Molloy contingent here today. That meant that if we won, we would play Hofstra on Sunday.

We won a tough game, and I walked upstairs after the game to say hello to my family and friends. I thanked Jeff Wilkins for coming, and hugged Dad. Coach Sutter emerged and came over to us. "I can't believe you're playing for St. John's, Billy, but I'm proud of you." He'd coached Jeff on JV the year before me, and Jeff respected him as a coach. Jeff played one year for Division Three Stony Brook without playing a minute on varsity at Molloy, but had to quit for money reasons. Coach Sutter was so happy to see all of us, and wished us good luck as he left Alumni Hall.

On Saturday night, Mom made a nice dinner in Rosedale for myself, Dad, Jeff, Timmy, and Greg. We ate like kings and went out together. I was the designated driver to Long Beach that night; we always had fun when the Rosedale crew got together. I got in touch with Pat Cosgrove and told him that it would be amazing if I got in the game against him on Sunday. I also congratulated him on his game-winning shot. He was excited for Sunday as well.

In my junior year at St. John's, I didn't really know anyone, so I hung out at Hofstra with Pat and his teammates. What a great group of guys. We had a lot of fun over the last year and a half, and this game would be no different. St. John's was favored because we were bigger and more athletic. The game was played in front of a big crowd, and there were lots of NYC and Long Island basketball players in the game. This is the difference between today and twenty years ago. We had eighteen players from the NYC area on both teams. Compared to the college game today, that's amazing. Playing at home in front of your family and friends was important. Playing at Madison Square Garden was important. Playing in the Big East was important. Today players go all over the country and play due to TV and Internet exposure. I played 53 straight games for Westbrook College in Maine, and I had a blast, but if I were a scholarship Division One recruit out of high school, I would have played for St. John's in Madison Square Garden. I wouldn't have looked at any other schools.

Sunday morning, I awoke to the banging of my mother's cane on the bannister leading upstairs to my bedroom. She had good news for me. Ever since I worked for the *Daily News* years ago, we had it delivered, and there was an article on the back page about walk-ons. Wayne Coffey had done a wonderful job capturing the life and job of a Division One basketball walk-on. He featured myself and Bradley, due to our common bond of never playing high school basketball.

Wayne wrote, "Mitaritonna might be the most selfless walk-on, and looked more like a bouncer than a basketball player." Very nice of him to say that about me. I was proud to represent all walk-ons around the country. There have been very few times in which I felt as fulfilled as a person as I did the morning of December 11th.

We played Sunday against Hofstra, and they were no match for us. Pat had a good game overall, but it wasn't enough. Coach Mahoney looked down at myself and Bradley, with two minutes to go in the game. As Bob Sheppard announced our names correctly, since we'd been added to the roster officially now, Pat Cosgrove was taken out by his legendary coach, Butch van Breda Kolff. I always wanted to cover Pat in a game, but I had the pleasure of guarding my other buddy, Matt Carpenter. On the next possession, Hofstra tried to press us, so we ran our press breaker. Bradley took it out and passed it to me, coming to the ball. The Hofstra guard went right back to Bradley because they thought I wouldn't dribble. I faked at him and dribbled the ball up myself. That five seconds of bringing the ball felt as free as I've ever felt on a basketball court. Nothing in front of me but daylight.

Two players came at me, so I dished to James Scott on the right wing. He did his best to get it back, but I didn't get a shot off because my friends on Hofstra were double-teaming me as a joke. Darius Burton, future Baldwin HS basketball coach who I would later compete against, guarded me tightly. It was very funny, but that left Bradley open and he nailed a three-pointer to get a nice ovation. We received wristwatches after the game, and Mrs. Cosgrove took a nice picture of myself, Pat, and John Mavroukas afterwards. Mr. Cosgrove yelled over to me with his raspy voice, "Way to go, Billy boy...the Last of the Redmen!" The announcers at MSG called me "Brian Mahoney's victory cigar," in honor of NBA Hall of Fame coach Red Auerbach, who always lit up a cigar at the end of a big win. This particular week in December was a whirlwind; I was starting to really enjoy my newfound fame.

At our next practice, Coach Mahoney came up to me and said, "Billy, you and Bradley are getting more publicity than the starters. I hope you're enjoying this. By the way, we're bringing you and Bradley on the road with us. Go see Dutch after practice for red uniforms."

I looked at Bradley and we high-fived each other. I whispered to him so no one could hear, "Bradley, we're going to Miami!"

Our next game would be on Saturday, December 18th, at the Nassau Coliseum against the Fordham Rams. It also happened to be finals week, so we were given a break to study. On Thursday, two days before our next game, Jenn Walsh convinced me to give blood after lunch. I told her that I had practice at 2:30, but she didn't care. I donated blood, went to practice, and was invited to a sorority function at Hofstra, so I knew I would be out with Matt Carpenter and Pat Cosgrove later on. It was a great night of dancing and drinking. We got back to their dorm at 2:00 a.m. after a fun night, and I passed out. I woke up at 6:00, drove home to Rosedale, and went up to bed.

The only problem was that I had a theology final at 9:00 and I hadn't set my alarm. It was 9:20 when Jenn Walsh called my house and spoke with my mom. Jenn spoke with the nun who was our professor, who said that if I didn't get there by 10, I would fail the class.

Mom used her cane and screamed for me to wake up. I ran out of the house and got to St. John's in twenty minutes. I sprinted into class at 9:55 a.m., grabbed the exam, and did the best I could. Jenn laughed at me for the rest of the test, because I looked like hell and was sweating profusely. She waited for me to finish and we went to breakfast. I told her it was a bad idea to give blood, but she continued to make fun of me.

We had practice early that day at 2:00 p.m., because we were going to stay at the Glen Cove Mansion the night before our game at the Nassau Coliseum. Thank goodness everyone was now healthy and they didn't need me in practice as much as usual. We got to the hotel, and since Bradley and I were travelling, we got to experience free food and meal money. We received dinner at the hotel, $20.00 for the meal, and a snack at night, all in accordance with NCAA rules. They kept us in a hotel the night before games on the road or day games at home to make sure the players would behave, which was very smart. I was in awe of how wonderfully we were treated, and I was very thankful to Coach Mahoney for his decision to bring me on the road.

The entire team got together, went bowling the night before the game, and had a lot of fun. Then we had to go to our rooms, and I was paired up with the most interesting player on the team, Sergio Luyk from Madrid, Spain. Sergio was a 6'9" shooter who'd learned the game from his dad, Cliff Luyk, who was the coach of Real Madrid in the top European basketball league. Sergio loved listening to his CD player with all kinds of music. He also loved the ladies, and his European charm was a big hit in New York. Every girl on the St. John's dance team knew Sergio. He knew once he left St. John's that he had a spot on Real Madrid, and this guy could shoot the ball. Sergio could be a game changer if he got hot.

This game was a part of a four-game lineup on a Saturday at the Nassau Coliseum. The NCAA tournament was going to host first-round games in March, so this was a test run. We played Fordham, and the game was relatively close until we opened it up late in the second half. With four minutes to go and the lead up to twenty, I heard the chants of, "WE WANT BILL! WE WANT BILL! WE WANT BILL!" My family and friends were pumping up the crowd, trying to get me into the game.

Coach Mahoney came down the sideline with 2:30 left and put Bradley in first. He got a very nice ovation, but the chants for me were starting to get louder and louder. My teammates Shawnelle Scott and Carl Beckett were now on each end of me, pulling my shooting shirt off. One player from All Hallows and one player from Christ the King, who'd beat up on Molloy while we were in high school and who I looked up to with great admiration, were now doing all they could so I could play for two minutes in a blowout win. Their efforts paid off, as the chants got too much for anyone to ignore. Coach Mahoney gave me my moment in the sun. He sent me to the table, and I could hear my friends and family cheering. Play went on for fifteen seconds as I waited patiently at the scorer's table. A Fordham player was fouled, and I was waved into the game. I ran onto the foul line area in position to box out, and I could clearly hear screaming from all of my Long Island cousins. The shot missed and the rebound came to me, but I was bumped as I tried to outlet the ball to Bradley. The ball fell forward and I picked it up to throw it again, but this time I rifled it up to Bradley, who caught it in stride and shot a three-pointer. SWISH!

Our teammates were cheering for him, and so was I. We were to keep our walk-on pact to only look for each other on the court. Fordham came down and hit a quick layup, so we got the ball up the court quick for one last look. Bradley threw it deep to me, but it was intercepted, and the game ended. It didn't matter because I got to play and we won. This was a good win for us going into our pre-Christmas game with Niagara.

On December 22nd, all of my friends were coming to the Niagara game because they were home from college. That meant we would go out afterwards and have a great time. I was very excited, because Niagara was not having a good year so far, and we were playing much better as a team. The day was like any other home game at Alumni Hall, except there were no students on campus. We had our pregame meal at Dante's, got our meal money, and walked back to campus with the team. I sprinted into the gym because I wanted to get free throws up before warmups. I had a very good feeling about this game.

The game started like any other, but I was able to make eye contact with Dad, Greg, Timmy, Walter, Gerry, and my other soft-ball buddies. Also in attendance were Joe Burns, Mike Gillespie, Joe Grimpel, Nick LaBella, and Pat Cosgrove, all from Molloy. I heard another screaming person yelling my name: Tom Greer, who was a Molloy manager like myself. He graduated seven years before me and chaperoned us on the Molloy basketball Myrtle Beach trip my junior and senior years. I saw him on the layup line and smiled back. He was so proud of me as a former manager. He was sitting with Coach Curran. The crowd was definitely in a positive holiday spirit.

This game went as expected. We got out to a huge lead and kept it well into the second half. As the four-minute TV timeout came close, Bradley and I were getting excited and prepared, and the chants of "WE WANT BILL! WE WANT BRAD!" coming from the student section were helping our cause. With two minutes left, Coach Mahoney put both of us in, and we looked at each other. We had a plan tonight. We were both going to score.

Play began with Niagara scoring quick, and we outletted the ball with no delay. I got the ball sprinting up the sideline to Bradley, and he was fouled going to the basket. He hit the first one and the crowd celebrated. Bradley smiled back at me and lined up for the second shot. The ball came off the rim and Niagara brought it up the court. They hit a quick jump shot and I took off down the left wing. Carl Beckett got the ball out quick to Brad, and he took one dribble and threw it up to me past half court. I had done this so many times before in my CYO days, Rockaway summer league games, and at Westbrook. I had my left hand up as always and caught the ball in stride. Without hesitation, I saw an opening to the basket, and something inside me said to take this opportunity with power and strength. I got to the basket in two dribbles and got blocked by the defending Niagara player, but I heard a whistle! The referee cut me a break and I was going to the line. The crowd erupted in cheers, and I did everything in my power to compose myself. I felt very similar to how I'd felt during the game at Maine Maritime at the end of my freshman year for Westbrook. There have been certain situations, as an athlete and coach, where everything slows down and goes quiet. This was one of the first times I experienced that on the court. I have learned to channel it today as a coach, but back then I was just starting to understand this inner power. Some people call it "the Zone" but I call it focus.

I went back to the free throw shooting routine my father had showed me in my backyard years before. There was no sound, only focus on the job at hand. The referee bounced the ball to me and I put my right foot on the nail on the court, which signifies the midpoint of the rim. My right foot, right knee, right elbow, and right hand were in alignment. My middle finger was on the air hole of the basketball as I made eye contact with the front of the rim. My routine was three dribbles, find the air hole once again, and make eye contact with the rim. The ball left my hand and it felt good. It had excellent arc and good follow through. SWISH! I did it. Years of being cut, defeated, told I wasn't good enough, all washed away with that one made free throw. It validated all the positive messages my father had given me: never quit, and never let anyone tell you that you're not good enough. As long as you think you can achieve a goal, it can happen. It also told everyone that I belonged. This was my time to shine, and I nailed it.

I must admit that the cheering from the crowd really got to me. I had to step off the line and compose myself in order to take the second shot. I felt accepted by the educated and passionate St. John's fans, as well as my family and friends. I took the second shot, but it bounced in and out. Tom Bayne, the redshirt freshman I'd worked out for four months the year before, put it back in. It didn't matter to me that I'd missed the second shot, because I was in the scorebook for the first time and would go down in the history books at St. John's. Play resumed and I must admit that I was fired up. The next play on defense I took a charge on a Niagara player, but there was no call. They scored and the ball was brought up the court by Bradley, and again he got it to me on the left side. I did something I had practiced at Westbrook so many times. I pump faked the shot and the Niagara player went up in the air. I dribbled past him, spun with my dribble past the next defender, and went up for an off-balance layup with an ugly shot off the backboard. But I still got a standing ovation. Who gets applause for a blown layup? WALK-ONS DO!

The game ended, and we went into the locker room. There, a few extra people were waiting to talk to the team. Walter Berry and Shelton Jones were talking with Coach Rutledge in the hall outside the locker room. They were two members of the 1985 Final Four team that I'd idolized growing up. As I entered the locker room, I noticed a tall and skinny young man named Felipe Lopez speaking Spanish with a big guy in a Mets hat. He turned to speak with me, and I realized it was Bobby Bonilla, All-Star outfielder for the Mets. As a big Mets fan, I went up to him immediately. Bobby stopped what he was saying to Felipe and gave me a big bro-hug to congratulate me on a great game. I was smiling ear to ear and thanked him. Felipe gave me a bro-hug as well, and I went to my locker. This night was surreal and only getting better. I sat down to try and absorb it as my teammates came up to me to congratulate me. It was nice to have their approval.

Bobby Bonilla sat down next to me after my shower, and we talked baseball for twenty minutes. I was the only one in the locker room who could talk baseball, and he was very knowledgeable about all sports. He left, and I went upstairs to meet with all of my friends and family in the Alumni Hall lobby. It was the first time in my life that I was the center of anything, and it felt amazing. The *Daily News* wrote the next day, "Walk-on Billy Mitaritonna, longtime Matt Brust fan, hit a foul shot for his first point." My friends and I had a great time that night, and it was right in time for Christmas.

As if the newfound fame and playing time weren't enough for myself and Bradley, Alex Evans surprised us with a second semester gift. A former men's basketball scholarship player named Mitchell Foster graduated in December, leaving a one-semester scholarship available. Alex spoke with Coach Mahoney, and they decided to award that scholarship to the two walk-ons. Bradley and I were to split the $4,500.00 tuition scholarship. They brought us into the basketball office to give us the good news, and we could not have been more gracious or honored. A classy move by Coach Mahoney and Alex Evans. They appreciated our efforts in a year when we expected nothing in return. It was an amazing feeling, and an honor to be so appreciated by the St. John's basketball program.

Over Christmas break, I started to read Pat Riley's book *The Winner Within*, and as someone who wanted to coach one day myself, I found it captivating. I still read it once in a while to get a new perspective on my coaching style. In his book, he talks of his coaching philosophy, handling a team of superstars, and something fascinating called the "Disease of Me." Coach Riley said the "Disease of Me" could ruin a season very quickly due to negative actions by one or more players. His theory was based on five players on a team each giving 20% of the effort to win. If one of the players believes that he should receive 80% of the rewards, this was counterproductive, and the team would fail. I found this interesting, since I'd played on several teams only to watch these teams self-destruct due to one player feeling he deserved all the credit instead of sharing. In our case at St. John's in 1993-94, there were a lot of players who wanted the spoils but did not deserve them. We had talent, but failed to have chemistry when it counted.

The tough part of our schedule was starting, and we left for the ECAC Holiday Tournament the day after Christmas in New York

City. For four days, we were going to be spoiled rotten by the people running the tourney. It was going to be great walking around the city, staying in a nice hotel, eating fancy dinners, going to a Nets-Knicks game, and playing at MSG. We received $20 per meal for four days and got fed every four hours. I really felt like a scholarship player with all of this attention. We played Fairleigh Dickinson in the first part of the doubleheader, and our team looked slow and sluggish. I'm not sure any of the players knew how nicely they were being treated by the ECAC committee. They took things for granted and didn't realize how very cool this was. Just three years earlier, I would receive $6 per meal at Westbrook and have to stay in motor lodges all over New England. As far as our team went, the walk-ons were a part of the team, but the scholarship guys were the ones people paid to see.

At the end of the FDU game, we were up big, and for the fifth time, Coach Mahoney played Bradley and myself. We had the honor to play in a building with so much history, where the Knicks and Rangers were having amazing seasons, and I fully appreciated the opportunity. (This wasn't like the Augusta Civic Center in Maine.) Anyway, I took some shots and got some applause for missing again, but it was okay because we won and got the opportunity to face Georgia Tech two days later. This was going to be a big test for us right before the two-month Big East regular season. We played an inspired game, but something was missing for us at the end of games. Shawnelle was a great inside presence, but playmaking guards are necessary to win in late-game situations. Also, I didn't feel we had good chemistry, and Pat Riley was right about the "Disease of Me" because it had started to creep into the fabric of our unit.

Lastly, we had a coach who was a defensive genius in Al LoBalbo, and our guys didn't buy into the system. I'm not sure if we didn't practice it enough, or if the players didn't want to play team defense, but I learned at Westbrook that everything starts with team defense. Your team cannot be successful unless you make a commitment to team defense and your coaches stress it daily. Coach Graffam would have been a terrific Division One coach if given the chance, and I believed in him and his system 100%. But I'm not sure our players bought into what our coaches were saying. I learned at age 21 that the direction of a team is directly in relation to its head coach. Coach Mahoney was a wonderful basketball coach, but sometimes you don't have the right players that buy into what you teach.

Our record at the end of the Fairleigh Dickinson game was 7-2. After losing to Georgia Tech, we lost the next four games to even up our record at 7-7. When we played the stronger, more experienced teams of the Big East, we couldn't finish the job. It was Friday, January 21st, and we were heading to Miami, Florida. This was going to be a fun trip. Everyone needed it badly, because it was a chance to get back in the win column. 85 degrees and sunny might help our spirits.

We practiced early in the afternoon and got on the bus heading to LaGuardia Airport. We were to eat when we touched down in Florida. As we waited for our flight, some of us decided to stop and pick up burgers in the airport. I was starving, so I grabbed airport food. Bad idea. We landed in Miami, and it was gorgeous weather. We had dinner at the hotel and then an early bed check. I left dinner not feeling great, went straight upstairs to throw up, and did that all night long. Food poisoning is not a pretty sight. My roommate Sergio called our trainer Ron Linfonte to check on me, and there was nothing anyone could do. I didn't fall asleep until 4:00 a.m., and I got up sweating and dehydrated. Sergio brought up some Gatorade and fruit for me from breakfast, but I was in agony. We had a late afternoon game, so we had a noon lunch and then got back to the room to grab our gear to be on the bus by 1:30. Before each game, Father Jim Maher would say Mass in a hotel room for the coaches or any of the players. I went to Mass for the first time all season, and the coaches started to get worried about me. Father Jim said a special prayer for me, and we left for the game. I felt just well enough to warm up, but I didn't take off my sweats for the game like everyone else did. I was still sweating and cramping up, but I had enough energy to cheer our team to its first win in January. We ran into the locker room and there were smiles for the first time in three weeks. The flight home was bittersweet, as I hadn't gotten to enjoy Miami. When I got back home Saturday night, my mother knew something was wrong with me, because she watched the game on TV and saw I did not take off my sweats all game. I couldn't believe she could tell that from TV, but mothers have special instincts about their children.

We were optimistic for the next two games, since we were playing at the Garden, but we got embarrassed by Boston College and absolutely crushed by Minnesota on CBS before the 1994 Super Bowl. The team captains, Carl and Shawnelle, called a meeting the day after the Minnesota game. The team was to shave their heads as a sign of team unity. I was willing to do it, but Mo Brown refused. He said, "White people don't look good bald. You can get a short haircut, but trust me, Bill." I must admit that Mo was a great teammate. He was also a winner, as he won the PSAL MVP and championship for Grady HS in Brooklyn in 1992. Mo had an excellent point guard head on his shoulders, but he had fallen out of grace with the coaches. He wasn't a great shooter, so other teams would drop off him, and he couldn't hit the three consistently. That hurt his confidence, and they put James Scott at the point. Something had to change, and quick.

We went down to Philadelphia to play Villanova and got there the night before. After a big breakfast, we left the hotel in the morning to go to the gym earlier than normal opponents. There was a reason for that, as the Villanova students were brutal when addressing the other team from the bleachers. We walked into the Pavilion early enough to miss the students. As our team warmed up on our basket an hour before the game, the students were let into their seats, and Shawnelle warned me about it on the bus. He said not to react to what you hear from the student section. They immediately went after Shawnelle, and a student threw an empty Dunkin' Donuts box onto the court. They were yelling obscenities, calling Shawnelle fat. He loved it and laughed it off. After a couple of minutes, they caught me rebounding for him and asked if Shawnelle could share his donuts with me for helping him out. They started making fun of my last name and asking if I was an American citizen. I found it hysterical, and we went inside for pregame. Our team played with more fire, but came up short. Villanova is a hard place to win.

But things started to change, as we won the next three games against Providence and Miami at home, and at Pittsburgh. On the day of the Miami game on February 8th, it snowed ten inches in NYC. Miami flew in the night before, but we were on fire. Sergio hit three three-pointers in the first half and we were rolling. This game was on ESPN, and maybe Coach Mahoney would put us in with two minutes left. This was a special game for me. Dad was able to get there straight from work to see me play against one of my high school friends who played at Miami.

Steve Frazier had been a scoring machine in high school. As a junior at Molloy, he scored over 400 points during the 1989-90 season. I had the pleasure of guarding him in every practice. Coach Curran liked me to play him because "I toughened him up." Steve was an amazing basketball player, but had problems academically at Molloy, so he transferred to Andrew Jackson for his senior year of high school. He averaged 40 points per game and got a scholarship to Miami. In his first practice at Miami during Midnight Madness in 1991, he tore his ACL dunking and was a medical redshirt in his freshman year. What a tough break for a nice kid.

Anyway, on this night he was now healthy and playing for Miami against us. As the game got out of hand, the ball went out of bounds, and Steve took the ball out in front of our bench. He looked at me with surprise and said, "Bill, I can't believe you play for St. John's." I said, "Thanks, Stevie, maybe I can guard you again one more time?"

Coach Mahoney walked down with two minutes left and put us in. But just like in the Hofstra game, the Miami coach, Leonard Hamilton, took out my friend Steve for the last two minutes. During my entry into the game, ESPN had a shot of the Miami bench, and Steve was absolutely shocked that I was in the game. I had a feeling of being a part of getting Steve ready for college, and now he was happy for me. He was always a class act. We spoke briefly after the game, and that would be the last time I would play for St. John's. (6 games, 12 minutes, 1 point.) I didn't know that at the time, but it didn't matter, because I was enjoying every minute of it.

Our season was looking up, as we got to 11-10 after we beat Pittsburgh. But it came with a price. Shawnelle dunked a ball awkwardly at the end of the game and landed on his thumb. It didn't look good, but he tried to play at Seton Hall later that week. It turned out that he needed surgery and his college career was over. He did score over 1,000 points for his career, but we were lost without him.

After losses to Seton Hall and Georgetown, we drove up to Providence and played badly against a team we should have beaten with Shawnelle. But two players stepped up in his place for the rest of the year, Sophomore Charles Mineland and Freshman Roshown McLeod. Charlie was an undersized post player with good range on his jump shot. He was a tough player to guard. Roshown was as smooth a player as I've ever seen, and the best video game player in my lifetime. His hand-eye coordination was off the charts. Roshown had pro basketball in his future. He was a deadly scorer. They both started to play well.

We got on the bus to drive home from Providence, and the players were allowed to bring a VCR tape of any movie they wanted to watch. The coaches would approve, and away we would go. Our coaches were so pissed off that they said no to every movie that was given. I had a popular movie with me, *Goodfellas*, one of my favorite films. Coach LoBalbo and Coach Mahoney turned around and said, "Finally, a good movie. Let's do it." Initially, the players weren't happy with me, but they got off the bus saying good job. Everyone enjoyed the film. It was a small win in a season going downhill.

On senior day in late February, I had a great day. We were to play Syracuse at noon at MSG, and St. John's was to honor the five seniors. It was also a special day because my good friend Joe Burns and his Manhattanville Valiants were to take on Stony Brook at the conclusion of our game. His team was on hand to watch our ceremony. An hour before the game, the Athletic Director Jack Kaiser and his staff were to bring the five of us out with our families. My dad got my mom in the car at 9:30 a.m. to start the trek into NYC. A part of my mother's medical condition was vertigo, as well as low blood pressure. On that day it kicked in, and they got as far as Queens Boulevard before Dad had to turn around. He had to bring Mom home and then sprint into Manhattan to get there by 11:00. She felt horrible and was in bed for days afterwards. I knew why she couldn't make it, but I was glad my dad got there in time. The staff waited for our families to get there and started at 11:30.

We walked out one by one, and when they called my name at Madison Square Garden with my father next to me, it was truly special. I was so proud that Dad could join me on the floor at the Garden. Now we both had the honor to play at the world's most famous arena. They gave us roses (which Dad brought home to my mother) and a wonderfully framed picture of each of us in a St. John's uniform. What a nice way to start off our matchup with Syracuse.

On that day, we played inspired and with great ability. Our upperclassmen were fired up, and Charles Mineland created havoc against the legendary Syracuse 2-3 zone. The game went back and forth, but a controversial call at the end sealed our fate. Lawrence Moten, who was their top scorer, was dribbling the ball in a tie game down into his corner, and lost his balance. The official called a foul on Derek Brown, who was guarding him tight, but replay shows that Moten fell out of bounds on his own and not due to a push. They gave him two free throws and we lost by two points. I was crushed because I thought our guys played tough. As we left the court, I ran into Joe Burns and his team waiting to enter. We chatted for a second and Jim Boeheim, the head coach of Syracuse, stopped, looked at us, and said, "Helluva way to make a living, huh, guys?" Neither of us knew what to say, but Joe ran out with his team and I went into the locker room to shower. I asked Coach Mahoney if I could stay and watch my friend's game, and he said yes. I sat behind the Manhattanville bench to cheer on Joe and his team to a big win at Madison

Square Garden. Joe hit two big foul shots at the end to win the game. We hit the Upper East Side bars with Joe and his team after the game. What a great night.

We finished the season with a loss to UConn in the Big East tournament and ended up 12-17. The worst record in the last 30 years at St. John's. I, like all the players and coaches, was exhausted. As we got on the bus ride home from MSG after our season-ending loss, Carl Beckett, Lee Green, and Shawnelle Scott were spoken about by the coaches with reverence and thanks. They were good guys from NYC who'd given their all to St. John's. I remember the bus leaving the Queens Midtown Tunnel and the beautiful blue sky as the sun was setting. It reminded me of the blue sky in Maine on my first day of college. I was able to reflect on my college basketball experience with a big smile. It was a quiet bus ride home, but what I learned about being a walk-on was simple. You have to be good enough to play, but also embrace your role as a bench player. There was a solid future to look forward to for the program, as two McDonald's All-Americans were coming next year, Felipe Lopez and Zendon Hamilton.

But there was a major change on campus. Rev. Harrington was the President of St. John's, and he was approached the year before by a Native American Congressman who was travelling across the country to ask schools and universities to change the nicknames of teams that were offensive. He felt that "Redmen" was offensive to Native Americans. Rev. Harrington could have said that we were the "Redmen" because we wore red shirts, like Syracuse wore orange and Duke wore blue. So Harrington made the announcement of the name change during our season and put out a survey to the student body to change the name. The survey read:

___ Red Lightning
___ Red Storm
___ Red Thunder
___ Other

. . .

GUESS WHAT A MAJORITY of the student body did? They wrote in REDMEN where it said other, and showed the student body was somewhat together. I'm not sure if anyone was truly happy with the change, but it did signify the end of an era. After all, St. John's had a tradition of excellence, academically and athletically. There are people all over NYC who still have season tickets to St. John's today because of Joe Lapchick, Lou Carnesecca, Chris Mullin, Malik Sealy, etc. That was why I went to St. John's. I wanted to be a part of that family of excellence. But it's almost like when they made the decision to change the name, the team and the school changed. So many people I have talked to about St. John's over the years are dying for a return to that time. We made it to the Elite 8 in 1999 with Ron Artest, Erick Barkley, and Bootsy Thornton, but since the 1992-93 loss to Arkansas in the second round of the NCAA tourney, the 1999 team has been the only time we made it to the Sweet 16. It's been over twenty years since I graduated, and the team hasn't had much success. But now our coach is the reason why I played basketball in the first place: Chris Mullin. He inspired me to play the game of basketball, and he's doing a great job bringing us back to national prominence. I'm ecstatic they hired him, and we will pray he can get it done.

CHAPTER NINETEEN

"TOGETHER"

I WENT to the St. Patrick's Day Parade in 1995 and had a blast walking up 5th Avenue to the Upper East Side. That's where I met up with Joe Burns, Pat Cosgrove, and Pat Hurley after work to have a fun night watching college basketball. I had just moved into a house in Long Beach, living the bachelor life, when I met the most important person in my life in the same neighborhood where my parents met. Kristen O'Donnell was an Upper East Side resident and the cousin of my very good friend Joe Burns. We met at the famous Irish pub Ryan's Daughter, which was located in the Yorkville section of Manhattan blocks from where my mother had grown up. After dinner, Joe introduced me to Kristen, but she wanted nothing to do with me. She was very attractive and caught my eye, but she'd just worked a long week as a mutual fund accountant, and she wasn't interested in a tipsy substitute teacher with no money.

Two weeks later, Joe Burns informed me that myself and Pat Cosgrove needed to rent a truck to move him from Rockaway to East 65th Street in Manhattan. I found it funny that Joe convinced us to do all this and promised dinner as a reward. We spent our day off driving into the city and moving him into his cousin's apartment building. That was the day I fell in love. His cousin, Kristen, found an apartment for Joe and Pat Hurley and came upstairs to welcome them. I was sitting on the heaviest pull-out couch in history, exhausted after carrying it up five flights of stairs, when she re-introduced herself. She had a radiant smile to go along with her beautiful blue eyes. Immediately I got the gut feeling that she was special. I've always listened to my gut, whether it was sports or life. Kristen's parents and Joe's family took us out to dinner, and I spent the entire night staring at her, but she never looked back at me. I was a little creepy, but I couldn't stop. We went back to Joe's apartment for drinks and she finally spoke to me. I made it clear I was interested and we hit it off immediately. I asked her if she was going to be in Manhattan the next weekend and if she wanted to go out with our crew for drinks. She agreed and that was it. We fell in love and we were married two years later. Together, we are a true partnership, and my professional success as a teacher and coach is directly related to her guidance, support, and love.

After two years of living in an apartment and saving money, we bought a house in May of 1999, and it was there that I got one of the most important phone calls of my life. A Long Island school district wanted me to teach social studies. It was my wife who encouraged me to take the interview, and the rest was history.

When I was hired to teach in 1999, at Half Hollow Hills HS West, I was asked by the Principal, Dr. Jim LoFrese, and Assistant Principal, Mr. Chris Alexander, if I coached a sport. I told them that I'd coached basketball in the past. Their eyes lit up, and they said there might be a spot for me at Hills West. They gave me the teaching job; I was to be the JV boys' basketball coach. After a season of working with my good friend and football coach at Hills West, Kyle Madden, I was given the varsity job in the spring of 2000. I was energetic, passionate, and excited to take over a program in disarray and turn it into a respectable program on Long Island. That was my goal for the program, but I had to get the players to buy into my motto, "TOGETHER." So I made up t-shirts for the kids and away we went. The fall of 2000 was exciting in our school, as the football team made the playoffs, and there was a new feeling of optimism in a school that had been below average in the 1990s. In my first meeting with the team, I made a broad statement that I wanted our program to be one of the most respected on Long Island. We had a lot of work ahead of us, but I was looking forward to building a program.

I used Coach Graffam's teachings of help-side defense, and Coach Curran's drills from Archbishop Molloy. When I look back now at myself as a 28-year-old coach, I had a lot to learn, but I had fire and a determination to succeed. Luckily, I had a supportive Athletic Director at Half Hollow Hills named Anne Dignam who believed in me and my passion to coach. I selected great PEOPLE for my early teams, not necessarily the best players. I've always believed in using sports to teach life lessons.

I had some very good players in my first five years, such as Stephen Bowen, who went on to become a scholarship football player at Hofstra University and then played ten years in the NFL for the Cowboys, Redskins, and Jets. But my coaching strategy was all wrong. I listened to random people on how to run a basketball team. I was great with the kids, and there was mutual respect, but what I did philosophically with my team was not working. I thought a coach should call a play and the players should execute it. But what would happen when it broke down? They seemed to play better when they didn't "think," rather just played freely and creatively. In our first five years, we reached the playoffs only once, in 2003. In three of the five years, we lost close games at home on senior night late in the season to miss the playoffs. It was heart-wrenching for me, and I couldn't explain it to my players anymore. I felt responsible for losing close games, that I was the common thread. But for the second time in my life, I was not going to let failure make me quit what I loved.

At the conclusion of the 2005 season, one of my closest colleagues, Kyle Madden, invited me to a student-exchange trip in Kuna, Idaho. We were to take fifteen Hills West students to live with fifteen families for a week. Before this trip, I had thoughts of quitting coaching, because I didn't know how to fix my coaching philosophy. My players always listened to me, but I was teaching them how to play the wrong way. In J.F.K. Airport, I found a book that changed my philosophy on coaching and how to teach the game of basketball to teenagers. The name of the book is *The Miracle of St. Anthony* by Bobby Hurley and Adrian Wojnarowski. Coach Hurley had been the head coach of St. Anthony in Jersey City for over forty years, and won over 1,000 games and a ton of championships. More importantly, he saved hundreds of kids from the streets and sent them to college using basketball. On the way to Idaho, I was fascinated by the teachings and philosophy of Coach Hurley and adopted three major concepts:

1. I needed to hold our players accountable. I put too much responsibility on myself for the team's failures, and I didn't hold the players accountable enough for their actions, on and off the court.
2. I had to build a culture of winning through competition. We needed to compete in practice every day, compete in the weight room, and compete in life using basketball. I had to create a refuse-to-lose mentality.
3. My basketball philosophy was ass-backwards. I needed to use a great defense to create easy offense. For five years, I thought the way to win was fine-tuned plays on offense. It should be players, not plays, that win games. I thought I was teaching help-side defense, but I refused to commit to it for an entire season.

I READ his book whenever I could during that week and took notes. Coach Hurley is extremely demanding, he loves teaching and helping young student-athletes, and he does it his way. As an added bonus, I was able to talk to coaches from the Kuna High School basketball teams who had won state championships. I asked them how to build a championship program, and the common theme to all of their answers was that you need kids that compete every day in practice and have a refuse-to-lose attitude. It takes years to build. These coaches kept telling me to challenge my players to do more out of season on their own to get better, as well as holding them accountable, as Coach Hurley does. I looked in the mirror and changed up what I was doing. Failure can be a positive motivator. I found out a lot about myself as a coach and teacher in February of 2005.

When we got home, I had a meeting with all returning players, where we would have weekly workouts in the gym and weight room. I created an atmosphere of accountability, and the players saw a change in my teaching of the fundamentals. The next thing I did was make a phone call to Coach Graffam up in Maine. I asked him if he had time to help me over the summer to teach help-side defense and shooting. With no hesitation, he agreed, and said, "We'll get it done, Billy."

In July of 2005, fifteen years after he'd recruited me, Coach Graffam came down to my summer camp for three days and put on a clinic for a group of middle school and high school underclassmen while I took notes. He outlined the Westbrook help-side defense, and how it leads to the fast break. Fifteen years later, he saved me again and changed my coaching philosophy forever. Those young players at summer camp became my first championship team three years later.

In the 2005-2006 basketball season, things didn't turn around right away. I started a youth movement of very talented and extremely competitive sophomores and juniors. I also looked at a very talented 8th-grader and put him on JV with the other group of young players. This six-foot-one 8th-grader was Tobias Harris, who currently plays for the Los Angeles Clippers in the NBA. My philosophy was now very different. We were going to put all our efforts into our "Hills West" help-side defense. The Hills West way was to hold teams to 45 points per game or less. My first year using this system took some time to teach to our young student-athletes. I did everything Coach Graffam taught me, but the results were not following. I started to second-guess myself. During the Christmas break, I brought up four underclassmen to the varsity team and blended them with older players who were ready to take the next step. We started the season with several losses, and in a fourteen-game season, we went 2-5 in the first seven games. But our team defense was slowly getting better. Now that we'd seen all seven teams on film, we could plan to beat them the second time around. I kept teaching our help-side defense in practice every day and focused on things we could control, like being in an athletic stance or rebounding the basketball. My theme was breaking teams down with our constant help-side defense, and due to the fact that we were in better shape than our opponents, they would break down in the 4th quarter.

The second half of the league season started with defeating our rival Deer Park, and getting wins over teams we'd lost to the first time around. We'd knocked Deer Park out of the playoffs the year before, and they were much more talented than us this year, yet we held them to 42 points. We hosted Riverhead and held them to 40 points. Next up was North Babylon, who beat us the first time, but we held them to 28 points in another win. At 6-6 with two games left, we had to win one more game to go .500 and get in the playoffs. We lost a game, and had to go to Deer Park on their senior night and win to get in. I remember the practice before we played them. I put all the responsibility on the players, stating, "How do you want to end your season?"

The game with Deer Park started, and our players were inspired and focused on helping each other on defense. There was no look of fear like in past years, only determination. We kept preaching putting all of our energy into helping on defense, and that would translate into easy baskets. And that's what happened in the fourth quarter. Our senior guards, John Campo and Ryon Khaleel, each held their man scoreless, and each scored a career high 17 points to lead us to victory. We held onto a close win and celebrated our playoff berth like winning a national championship. It took me six years to figure it out, and I was thrilled. We went 7-7 to make the postseason tournament. We were able to sneak in the playoffs with an average team, and I learned so much from this .500 season.

First of all, our defense took two and a half months to teach, and I realized that if you stick with it and teach it correctly, a team will get better by the end of the season. Secondly, our help-side defense created unselfish play on offense. The theory is, if you help each other on defense, you will help each other on offense, and team chemistry will develop. And lastly, if you believe in a philosophy that promotes teamwork or defense or running the break, etc., sell it to your players and stick with it for the entire season. You can go back after the season and look at film to see where you can make it better for next year. For my first five years coaching high school basketball, I had no philosophy and changed up my schemes weekly. This confused my players and created doubt in my coaching ability. The 2005-06 season was the start of twelve consecutive playoff appearances, and even though we lost in the first round, it was the beginning of a championship team gaining much-needed confidence. As a coach, this team will always make me look back and smile. Even though we were a .500 team, I personally considered it a success.

The kids weren't the only people that needed confidence. I was so happy for them, and the way they refused to give up late in the season. Maybe losing four out of my first five years was a way of motivating me, like being cut in high school. I'm a big believer in things happening for a reason. Failure, again, was a major motivator for me in my professional life.

That next year, we went 13-7, and our young team gained valuable game experience that would help us in the future. Stepping up to lead us in scoring was the freshman named Tobias Harris. He'd grown from 6'1" as an 8th-grader to 6'6" as a freshman. He averaged 21 points per game, though he was surrounded by a very competitive group of juniors and seniors. They learned how to depend on each other offensively and defensively. We lost in the first round of the playoffs, but I felt good about our chances going into the offseason.

CHAPTER TWENTY

"OFFENSE SELLS TICKETS BUT DEFENSE WINS CHAMPIONSHIPS"

HOW DO you create a championship team? That was the question I asked myself in the offseason leading up to November of 2007. We had never gotten out of the first round of the playoffs since I was head coach. In my mind, we had all the pieces to make a run this season. My very good friend from Westbrook College, Beanie Soto, came to a lot of our games because he had gotten married and moved to Suffolk County. There's not a more loyal and supportive friend than Beanie. He would go out after games with myself and my assistant coaches to break down our performance. Beanie has always had a way of seeing specific details and turning them into a positive message. He and I definitely learned that from Coach Graffam.

Along with Beanie, Kyle Madden and my new volunteer assistant and Hills West alum Bryan Dugan were great in helping me game plan and scout our opponents. The coaching staff was in place—we had talented players, and our administration and teachers were supportive 100%. Now it was my turn to get this team to the next level. I re-read *The Winner Within* and *The Miracle of St. Anthony* before the season. I attended several preseason clinics with Villanova head coach Jay Wright, former Knicks coach Jeff Van Gundy, and

Bob Hurley. I spent a lot of time in the weight room with our players who didn't play a fall sport. But this squad had a special quality I had never seen in my program before. They hated losing more than they liked winning. This group was super competitive and refused to lose in any sport they participated in. Both our football team and soccer team went deep into the playoffs in the fall of 2007, so I had to wait for them to finish their seasons to start practice. Some coaches would find that annoying, but I feel winning carries over from season to season. We're lucky to have winning coaches who support each other. Our varsity football coach, Kyle Madden, coached JV basketball. Our varsity baseball coach, Tom Migliozzi, coached JV football and did the scoreboard for basketball games. Our varsity soccer coach, Doug Gannon, coached middle school basketball and JV baseball. Our varsity lacrosse coach, Nils Haugen, coached JV football and was the lead chaperone for all basketball games. It was important for the varsity coaches to help each other out, and in 2007-08, winning in soccer and football started us off on the right foot for basketball season. I made a competitive schedule that started later on in December, so we could get our football and soccer players into shape.

We had a solid core of six seniors, made up of the forwards Alex Aurrichio and Mike Meglio, and the guards John Conneely, Will Hennep, Cory Knox, and Steven Rollino. These six players knew their roles and refused to lose, and that allowed our team to succeed. Their job was to get our sophomore superstar forward the ball in position to score, as Tobias Harris was now 6'7" and an explosive scorer. He would average 29 PPG and score 726 points in 25 games. Our seniors knew he was our meal ticket.

Tobias had a diverse offensive repertoire. His shooting form was smooth and effortless. His jump shot was outstanding and the best I'd ever seen. Tobias could use his size down low in the post to be very effective inside. He worked out every day to get to this point. But his greatest attribute was his basketball IQ. Tobias was another coach on the court, and I can see him coaching after his playing career is over.

My plan for this year was very simple. We were going to "Control

Today." What does that mean? I learned that there are things in life you CAN control and things in life you CANNOT control. Knowing I had a veteran squad, we sat down as a team and came up with a list of Control vs. Cannot Control.

AN EXAMPLE FOR HIGH SCHOOL BASKETBALL:

CONTROL:

Layups, free throws, energy, hustle, help on defense, taking charges, conditioning, smart passing, and rebounding.

CAN'T CONTROL:

Bad weather, illness, injuries, referees, the crowd, shooting percentage, the other team, the other coach, family emergencies.

THIS LIST WOULD HELP us meet our daily goals in practice to get better. If something out of our control occurred, we would adjust to it and move on.

Before the team was selected, each player would have to run two miles on the first day of tryouts in under thirteen minutes. If a player completed the run, they wouldn't have to do the extra running after each tryout. We had to get in basketball shape, so I put them through our Conditioning Stations, like Coach Graffam had done to us years ago. These stations created a bond with our twelve-man roster instantly each day. Our squad bought into our philosophy early on, and I was now able to make a statement that my team absolutely loved and respected. I'm not sure if too many coaches are confident enough or trust their players enough to say what I said to them.

It was the week after conditioning stations, and we had scrimmages coming up on the schedule. I did two things that my players still talk about today. First of all, I came up with a saying about where we wanted to be as a team by the end of the year. I pointed to the county championship wall and said, "In order to get on that wall..."

I then pointed to the league championship wall and said, "You have to get on that wall first." Our short-term goal was to win the first league championship in fourteen years at Hills West, which would put us in line for a high playoff seed.

Secondly, I made a statement that I stuck with the entire season. I made this statement because I trusted their ability to play together and unselfishly.

"Guys," I said, "I tracked on film the amount of set plays we used in games in the last two years, and our success rate was awful. Therefore, we are not running any plays this year. As long as you play great Hills West team defense and run, I don't care what you do on offense, as long as it's unselfish."

They instantly smiled and started to pat me on the back with joy. Senior Cory Knox said, "Coach, that's the best thing you've done with us in three years."

Senior John Conneely spoke up. "We know our jobs, so let's go out there and do it. Remember, offense sells tickets but defense wins championships." He was absolutely right. We used that mantra throughout the season, as well.

We started off the season with wins over Northport, West Hempstead, and crosstown rival Hills East. We pressured every team with our help-side defense, and made teams give in to our philosophy of great defense so we could run the break unselfishly. We knocked off St. Anthony's of Huntington in a showcase game for Suffolk County public school bragging rights. Then we had to travel to Bellport right before Christmas for our first league game. The trip out there was usually miserable, and always a long night. But our team didn't care, as we steamrolled them in the first three quarters for a 25-point win. In the third quarter, we scored 28 points, all off our defense in transition. It was a great teaching point the next day in our film session. We went on to dominate our league, and our team was able to win all close games due to our defense. Tobias Harris' 29 PPG didn't hurt either. Our core of six seniors knew their roles, as John Conneely and Steve Rollino led us in assists, Alex Aurrichio and Mike Meglio controlled the boards, and Will Hennep and Cory Knox could lock up anybody in Suffolk County. We were a well-oiled machine, and we got to the last home game of the season senior night 17-0, hosting Riverhead, who we'd scored 90 points against the first time around. But this night was special. We were not fighting to get in the playoffs anymore, but actually enjoying the night honoring our loyal and supportive class of 2008 families.

Tobias Harris gave up his starting spot to Cory Knox on senior night, and I was so impressed. Tobias understood the importance of giving a loyal teammate a chance to play. I might be Catholic, but karma played a role on that night. We got off to a big lead before Tobias entered the game—Riverhead was having problems handling our pressure, so we got a lot of easy looks at the hoop through the first three quarters. We started the fourth quarter up 20 points, and I gave our team manager a uniform to wear before the game. Phil Sookram was an undersized young man, but he had a big heart and never missed a practice or game in three years. He had done everything from videotape games to run the clock in practice. I felt obligated to give him a chance to play. Tobias was on his way to a career night, with 35 points going into the fourth quarter. Riverhead kept fouling him, but he was a 90% free throw shooter; he made his living from the foul line. Coach Dugan went over to the scorer's table with four minutes left, and Tobias had 45 points. I left him in for one more minute up 25 points to get 50, but after that, I took him out at a career-high 47. He begged me to go back in with three minutes left, but I said it would be bad sportsmanship. He understood and sat right next to me, just in case I changed my mind.

At the three-minute mark, the crowd started to chant, "WE WANT PHIL! WE WANT PHIL!"

I laughed out loud and flashed back to my St. John's days. I looked at Phil and put him in with the reserves. He was so excited as play began. Our guys tried to get him the ball, but he was being double-teamed by the Riverhead players. Phil is 5'5", 140 pounds, and a great person, but not a great basketball player. On one possession, they bumped him while taking a shot, and there was no foul called. I asked a Riverhead player while he was by our bench why they were double-teaming Phil, and the kid said, "My coach said if the little kid scores, he's throwing us off the team. I'm sorry, Coach."

I replied, "Don't worry about it. It's not your fault."

I turned to Tobias, and he looked back at me with a serious look on his face. I knew what that look meant. He wanted to help Phil. I said, "Go get 50 and make sure Phil gets the ball."

He smiled and said, "I got you, Coach."

Tobias re-entered and immediately put in a three-pointer to get to 50. Riverhead missed the next shot and fouled Tobias as he was getting a rebound. He made both free throws and got Phil the ball on the next possession so he could get some shots up on senior night. Even though Phil did not score, our team was so excited for him. He deserved to play on senior night for his three years of dedicated service to our program. Tobias finished with a school-record 52 points, coming off the bench on senior night. I knew we had a special thing going now, and it was my job to keep the outside influences away from our undefeated season.

In the game of high school basketball today, there are so many outside influences. AAU coaches, sneaker deals, travel teams, agents, handlers, college scholarships, friends, and families can interrupt, or in some cases, ruin a team's chances for a successful season. I have dealt with all of these situations at various times in my coaching career. Outside influences can make or break the chemistry of a team, especially if friends or family feel they have the right to make changes. As a coach, it's a delicate balance, dealing with families and people who feel they're entitled to influence what happens on the court. My job is to teach life lessons using the game of basketball. Student-athletes have a lot on their plate without worrying about nonsense off the court. High school coaching is an art, and a big part of that is getting a group of teenagers to buy into a philosophy while being distracted by girls, social media, girls, iPhones, girls, the college search, girls, etc. It's hard enough without being pressured by parents about playing time or shot selection.

In the 2007-08 season, we faced more pressure, as our winning streak got larger heading into the playoffs. Then the interference started. I got a phone call from a parent asking about my half court offense, and telling me I should play zone defense. Another parent asked about his son's playing time. We were 19-0 and I was getting criticized by people outside the team. Again, it's a delicate balance, because if I didn't take a call from a parent, I would get an email from an administrator instructing me to meet with them. This is not something you want to deal with as you plan for the playoffs. As a coach, I'm charged with the task of coaching and protecting my players, and teaching my team how to win together. I do not coach parents, I do not coach uncles, and I do not coach older brothers. But it seems whether you win championships or lose a lot of games, coaches get phone calls from parents. We need administrators to create criteria to make sure coaches can work without interruption, in order to coach the way we want to coach. Outside influences can destroy a great season.

February of 2008 was a very stressful month for me. We went into the Suffolk County playoffs 19-0, and we were awarded the #1 seed for the first time in recent history. Also, we won a league title for the first time in fourteen years, and we had never made it out of the first round of the playoffs. We were the hunted, and I had one strategy to handle that. Do what we do every day in practice, and then do it in games. In other words, "Control Today." Our three-year experiment with this group was now going to be tested.

We won our first game over Connetquot over the winter break in

February on Tuesday. My assistant coach, Bryan Dugan, called a friend and found out we were playing league rival Bellport for the third time at home. He then pointed out the old-time quote: "Coach, it's hard to beat someone three times in a season." I didn't agree with that statement, because we had never been in the second round of the playoffs before. In my practice on Wednesday, we watched film of the previous game with Bellport at home, where they guarded our super-star sophomore Tobias Harris with two players all over the court. I instructed our core of six seniors that it was time for them to step up. Tobias was averaging 29 points per game, and our team did a great job of buying into my philosophy of help-side defense leading into fast break offense. This team, more than any team I had, could help on defense and pass unselfishly on offense. There were times that we looked like Magic Johnson's Lakers of the 1980s. But the playoffs are a different set of circumstances. Our practice on Thursday during the break was tense, and I wasn't happy with it. That will happen in a year when you've won twenty straight games. We finished practice early and got them in the huddle to break down. I told them that we did not control what we could today, and with the snow coming tomorrow, we might not play until Saturday afternoon. We left, and I knew that if we won the next game, we would be relaxed and excited to play at Stony Brook. But it snowed and snowed, and all playoff games were moved back to Saturday at noon. This was where the pressure got to me. I got home early Thursday afternoon, and my wife ran to work for the afternoon. Being at home with three young kids under the age of seven and sitting there, just thinking about the next game, can drive a person batty. Going through lineups, matchups, watching film, and not thinking of my family. Friday came, and the same pressure existed, but now I was taking it out on my family with a short temper.

After the snow fell on Friday, my wife went to work in the after-noon again, and I was slowly feeling the pressure. What some teachers and administrators don't understand is that while they're in Florida or on a Caribbean cruise, playoff basketball coaches work on the Thanksgiving, Christmas, and Winter breaks. During that week off, you have very little time to spend with your family. And high school basketball coaches don't coach for money, because there is very little.

Saturday morning came, and I left home early to set up the Hills West gym, as I always do. I love my family with all of my heart, but I needed a break. Our pregame shootaround was loose, and we were confident. The game was tight in the first half, and we were down double digits for the first time all year in any game. We cut the lead to six at the half, and I didn't have to say a thing in the locker room. My seniors took over the speech and the game in the second half. In the third and fourth quarters, we outscored them 49-24 and ran away with the game. We did something as a team after shaking Bellport's hands. In the locker room, I grabbed a pair of scissors and told them to follow me. We went out to the far side basket in the gym, and we all took turns cutting down a piece of the net. The kids didn't realize that would be the last time we would play at Hills West, after three years of hard work and dedication. As each player took a turn, the weight of the world left my shoulders slowly, and I felt relief. I knew we would play well at Stony Brook University if we got there. Tuesday night would be a lot of fun.

In fact, Monday and Tuesday were exciting for our whole student body. We created a buzz, and there was nothing more exciting than playing at a university gym in front of your fans. School was back in session, and everyone was talking about our semifinal matchup. I had a gut feeling we would play confident and inspired, and we did. Alex Aurrichio had 18 points and 22 rebounds, and John Conneely almost had a quadruple-double. He was playing on another level: 11 points, 13 assists, 8 rebounds, and 6 steals. Amazing numbers for two senior high school basketball players. We defeated Brentwood easily, and our opponent would be a perennial playoff contender, the Wildcats of Walt Whitman High School, coached by the legend Tom Fitzpatrick. We met on Wednesday to discuss our last game, and our guys were already talking matchups with Whitman. This was their CYO rival, who they knew better than any team in Suffolk County. We did have one issue with John Conneely, who was bent over in pain on the sideline with a stomach virus. I called his mother, and she picked him up so he could go home and rest. We didn't need him today, we needed him Friday night at 9.

The next three days at West were the reason you want your team in the finals. The players were the kings of High School West. Though they did enjoy the attention, it was my job to keep their heads focused. But I was still worried about John, who didn't come to school on Thursday, and that was rare. I called Mrs. Conneely, and she said she was getting him a doctor's appointment. That was a good thing; maybe they could give him fluids and get him ready. Our playoff practices were short, and that was done to keep us fresh and in rhythm. I gave Steven Rollino some extra reps at point guard for his sake, not mine. I knew he would be a more-than-adequate replacement if John felt sick during the game. Everyone knew John would not miss this game for anything.

On that Friday morning, February 29th (Leap Year), I was home for my daughter Courtney's preschool winter concert and got a phone call from John Conneely's mother, Joyce. I stepped outside into the cold to speak with her.

She said, "Hi, Coach, how are you?"

I replied, "Good. How is John feeling?"

"Coach, we're at Good Samaritan Hospital with John. We have been here all night. They diagnosed him with appendicitis, and he has surgery tonight at 6."

I almost passed out when I heard that, but said, "Oh my goodness, is there anything we can do? I feel so bad for John; he has looked forward to this for three years."

Her voice started to shake a little. "That's all he's talking about. He wanted to play and do the surgery in the morning, but he is in agony. I feel so bad for him, but we know everything will go well with his surgery."

I asked her if I could tell the team, and she agreed that would be the best thing right now so he wouldn't be inundated with calls. I left off that I would call him in the afternoon because he was asleep. I hung up and went into the concert, where my wife was waiting for me as the show was starting. I told her the news, and she grabbed my arm gently with concern and asked if John was going to be okay. But I could tell she really wanted to say something else. That something else was, "I can't believe this is happening to you and your team on the day of the Suffolk County Championship at 22-0."

My most important job of the season was telling John's two best friends when I got back to school at 11:00 a.m. I gathered his two buddies, Alex and Steven, to tell them the news. The main office paged them down to my basketball office in the boys' locker room. This was going to be hard, but I always talked about the difference between things you could control and things you couldn't. Injuries and illnesses were a part of sports, so there was nothing we could do but move on.

Alex and Steven came into my office with big smiles on their faces, but when they saw my facial expression, that quickly changed. I told them the news, and their expressions were of concern and shock. They asked if he was going to be okay, and if it was a routine surgery. I told them yes, and that he would be fine in a couple of days, but he was out for tonight. After the kids got a handle on his surgery, I spoke to Steven and said, "There was a reason for you to be here tonight. There was a force bringing you back to West after three years of Catholic high school. John is one of your best friends, so what an honor it would be for you to play your heart out for him."

Steven smiled, got up, and said, "I got this, Coach."

I replied, "I believe you, Stevie," and they walked out together.

The boys came to my classroom later in the day to tell me they were going to visit him and then come back for the bus. What a great idea for our team to visit John. They were truly "Together."

We played that night with all of our heart and talent. Forward Mike Meglio scored the first seven points of the game for us. Tobias Harris was the game-leading scorer with 19 points, hitting his last ten free throws in a row. Steve Rollino played an almost flawless game at point guard and did it with fire and passion. Will Hennep put the game away by hitting a three-pointer with 1:30 left, and Alex Aurrichio did his normal rebounding and scoring with a huge steal to ice the game. As time wound down to zero, we celebrated and jumped up and down like we'd won the World Series. These guys deserved it, but it was not fair to have John in the hospital. He was a huge reason why we'd got there, and I think we would have won by a larger margin if he was healthy.

But I kept thinking there's a reason for everything in life, and God put Steve here for this situation. Our team worked so hard for three years, and this proved that our philosophy on how to play the game of basketball was successful. February 29th, 2008 was a magical day for me. It reminded me of a night in Rockaway Beach during July of 1990. My parents always said good things happen to good people, and I sincerely believe that.

CHAPTER TWENTY-ONE

REACHING NEW HEIGHTS

A SEASON LATER, in 2008-2009, I had no returning starters due to graduation, and Tobias Harris transferred to Long Island Lutheran, so I had to rebuild very quickly. We had three seniors who'd been on the team the year before, a few underclassmen who showed promise, and a very talented freshman named Emile Blackman Jr. In my seventeen years as head coach, I've only had three players talented enough to play varsity basketball as a 9th-grader. The aforementioned Tobias Harris, Emile Blackman Jr., and in my later years, Cameron Jordan. All three ended up playing Division 1 athletics, Tobias and Emile for hoops and Cameron as a wide receiver for Syracuse football. Emile has basketball in his blood. His dad was a standout for Bishop Loughlin and Dowling College in the 1980s. Emile's mother, Ana, has a brother named Mark Jackson who played at St. John's and was a legendary NBA point guard. I made a decision in the preseason to put Emile on varsity, because it was time to start fresh and he was the best player in the gym, but I never told him that. Before I did, I called his mother Ana and asked if she thought it would be good for him socially and academically. She had a little apprehension, but after speaking with her son, she agreed.

I brought Emile in with my assistant coach, Bryan Dugan, and we told him of the great responsibility this would carry. He had no idea what we were talking about, because he was fourteen and flying by the seat of his pants. I had no clue what I was doing my freshman year emotionally either, and I got cut from the freshman team at Molloy. I was now asking Emile to be the man on a team with zero varsity playing experience. I must admit that I was riding the championship wave from last season, and conceded quietly to my assistant coach behind closed doors that we were not repeating as Suffolk County champions. But as a coach, you never express anything to the kids but winning the state championship, no matter the odds.

I knew we had to get back to our defensive basics, such as teaching an athletic stance and communication. In the 2005-06 season, when I started this new defensive philosophy, it took two full months of six days a week with film work to get our guys fully on board and performing at a high level. It was going to be a long road, but we were excited for this new group. I brought up Emile and three talented sophomores in wing Chris Cox, forward Chris Kaimis, and point guard Anthony Rollino. With those four athletic underclassmen, I knew we had potential to do well again in the future.

We had our first home game against Lawrence-Woodmere Academy, which I scheduled thinking I was going to have a stronger team. Something happened in the fourth quarter that we had not seen a lot in the Hills West gym. Emile dunked the ball, but he was fourteen years old. It was a powerful slam and our bench went crazy. He was our offensive leader in game one, and junior shooting guard Aaron McCree showed his ability to hit shots and guard the other team's best player. I now had some youth to work with. Senior guards David DiMaria, John Matzelle, and Gerard Lloyd from last year gave us some leadership, but it was hard in the beginning to get them to understand that I was going to give the underclassmen considerable playing time. Pat Riley's "disease of me" started to show with our older players. The seniors felt that they had paid their dues, and now it was their turn to play. That's not how it works in a competitive team setting, but I was sensitive to their loyalty to our program. Meanwhile, I got an interesting message from Tobias Harris in late December, telling me that he hated Lutheran and wanted to transfer back to Hills West after the New Year. The return of Tobias to our roster would be a game-changer, to say the least. Over the month of December, we started the league season 1-1, and our team would have to go .500 to make the playoffs.

After Christmas, we suffered some injuries and illnesses, so I went with a young lineup in a league game: freshman Emile Blackman, and sophomores Chris Cox, Chris Kaimis, Anthony Rollino, and junior Aaron McCree. This starting five had something in common. Each one showed me a competitive fire that was rare in high school athletics. In the back of my mind, I knew we could have the makings of a great team. January came, and Tobias decided to stay at Lutheran until the end of the season. His brother Tyler started to play well in his absence, so he felt obligated to finish the season with him. But Tobias expressed to me that he might finish at Hills West for his senior year, so I went with the young guys to get them experience.

In the first half of the league season, we went 1-5, and things were not looking good. We had our lowest point on MLK weekend, losing on a Saturday morning to West Babylon by ten points. The seniors were being childish about playing time, and the young guys didn't have a clue what was going on, so I used the midterms break to re-teach our help-side defense for four days. Some coaches would punish players in that situation, but instead I used it as a time to reflect and educate. Like 2006, the team bonded around our defense and we gelled as a unit. We knocked off four teams that we'd lost to the first time around, giving up less than fifty points per game. We defeated West Babylon on Senior Night as our seniors came around to buying into our philosophy. We made the playoffs at 6-6, and the future was bright for next season.

In 2009, my family started a tradition during the spring break week. We would take a family vacation to the Atlantis in the Bahamas. These were special times with my wife and children.

When we look back now, these were some of the best times we had as a family. On this trip, we travelled home through the Nassau Airport, and the Syracuse men's basketball coach, Jim Boeheim, was walking through customs behind my family. My three-year-old son Brendan was climbing all over me during the customs screening process. Coach Boeheim was on the phone behind me, and Brendan was jumping on my back, bumping into Coach. I turned and apologized to him, and he replied, "Don't worry about it. I have a young son too. That's what boys do."

I laughed and said, "Sorry again, Coach."

Then Coach Boeheim surprised me with his next statement. "We'll be down to see you next week. Tobias' father wasn't happy with Lutheran. Yeah, Dad wasn't happy. We'll be down to see him next week." Coach Boeheim saw my Hills West basketball shirt and with that, I found out that Tobias Harris was re-entering Hills West the following week. I didn't know because my cell phone had been off for five days. When we got back to New York, I got a text from Tobias saying he and his brother Tyler would see me Monday morning in the guidance office.

Monday came, and there they were, standing in the main lobby. Two young men who were 6'8" and their dad, signing them up for classes. This was a nice surprise, to see them smiling and waving hello to their buddies in the halls. Mr. Harris said fifteen college coaches were coming to see them work out the next three nights, so I had some phone calls to make. First up was our Athletic Director, Joe Pennacchio, to reserve the gym and ask him to stop by during these weeknights to talk to the coaches that were coming by. Next, I left a message for Coach Curran at Molloy to see what kind of workouts I should do each night for the coaches. You have to know Coach Curran to understand what he said, in his sarcastic tone: "Billy, you could do layups for an hour. They wouldn't care. All they want the kid to know is that they're there to see him practice. Remember, these guys wouldn't give you the time of day if you saw them on the street. It's a business. Always realize they're trying to get this kid by any means necessary." Coach Curran had a way of capturing the truth with his "straight shooter" way of speaking, and he was so right.

On Monday night, six big-time college coaches showed up to see Tobias work out. It went well, but a lot of people might not understand how much of a difference Tobias made. Two weeks earlier, I'd been the coach of a 7-13 squad with one junior, three sophomores, and a talented freshman who was our leading scorer. Now we had a highly recruited, big-time Division One All-American, and his very good 11th-grade brother Tyler added to the mix. The other thing people don't see is that coaches do not get paid to handle the recruitment of a high school player. I stayed after school for three days in April until 6 p.m. and ran workouts until 8. Coaches don't get paid to run workouts, answer phones on off periods, take meetings during the summer with parents, answer emails from college coaches, or do any other jobs that come about from this process. I estimated that I took over 600 phone calls from college coaches in the recruitment of Tobias Harris, and I didn't even get a t-shirt out of the deal. College coaches don't care about me or my team, only Tobias. As a high school coach, you realize that you have a responsibility to help your players in any way possible, but this was an extraordinary process.

Tobias' recruitment ran from April of 2009 all the way until November. During the fall, we had a lot of big-time college coaches visiting Hills West. Each day I was fielding multiple phone calls about our workout schedule and talking about Tobias the person, as well as faxing out his unofficial transcript. Every off period during the fall of 2009 was spent preparing his recruitment. Lunchtime would include grabbing food from the school cafeteria and walking with it to my basketball office, to eat on the run. Four days a week, we would have a different coach show up after school, or I would stay late at night to open the gym so Tobias could be seen by coaches who came in the evening. John Calipari and Rod Strickland of Kentucky, Rick Pitino and Ralph Willard of Louisville, Norm Roberts of St. John's, Paul Hewitt and Peter Zaharis of Georgia Tech, Keith Booth and Rob Eshan of Maryland, Jim Boeheim, Mike Hopkins, and Johnny

Murphy of Syracuse, Bob Huggins and Larry Harrison of West Virginia, and Bruce Pearl and Tony Jones of Tennessee were all in the Hills West gym together as a strength and conditioning coach worked out our guys. I was able to walk around and talk to the coaches. This was good, because I was able to catch up with Norm Roberts of SJU, who'd worked at Molloy twenty years ago. He was a class act. I was also able to speak with Coach Calipari and Rod Strickland. Coach Calipari brought Tobias and I into the computer lab to show us film of a recent practice where he pointed out where Tobias would fit into his offense. They were very polite and respectful in the recruitment of Tobias. Coach Pitino and his assistant Coach Willard sat with Emile Blackman's uncle Troy Jackson, who'd played at Louisville, and talked of Emile's athleticism and future in college basketball.

It was a pretty hectic fall season, as Tobias finally made the decision to narrow his recruitment to five teams: Kentucky, Tennessee, Louisville, Syracuse, and West Virginia. He was going to make a decision in the early signing period in mid-November. Now coaches were calling every day. Bruce Pearl got Peyton Manning on the phone and Bernard King on campus to recruit Tobias. Rick Pitino made several stops to his old stomping grounds on Long Island and just showed up to our gym. I was out watching a Monday Night Football game, where the Jets were playing the Dolphins in mid-November, when John Calipari texted me and asked to talk about Tobias. I went outside at halftime and called him back. Over the next ten minutes, he pleaded with me to talk to Tobias on his behalf the next morning. Tobias didn't let on what school he was going to choose, but rumors were spreading that he was leaning towards Tennessee. Calipari heard this, hence the phone call. I went back into the bar, and my college friends Walter Johnson and Ernie Hambrock asked me who was on the phone. When I told them it was John Calipari, they didn't believe me; it was very funny.

The buzz about our team reached a fever pitch during the preseason of the 2009-2010 season. As I was trying to piece together a squad, Tavon Sledge transferred into Hills West. He was a point guard from St. Benedict's Prep who'd moved with his father to Long Island. Tavon was 5'7" but the quickest and most explosive player I had ever seen. He came to an early workout after school and dunked the ball on his first possession. Everyone in the gym said, "Wow!" Now we had an All-American candidate in Tobias, his 6'9" brother Tyler, and point guard Tavon Sledge added to our core returning players of Emile Blackman, Anthony Rollino, Chris Cox, Aaron McCree, and Chris Kaimis. This was a solid eight-man rotation. When word got out about our potential All-Star lineup, the media (newspapers and websites) started to come around and call. I thought my job would get easier when Tobias announced he was signing with Tennessee, but it actually got busier when our season finally began. Every off period was spent calling someone from the media, preparing for practices, and dealing with parents. We scheduled a media day where all members of the local press and TV would interview myself and our players. Bob Herzog and Gregg Sarra from *Newsday* came to do a story, as well as Andrew Rappaport from *News 12 Long Island*. They asked me a question that I was prepared for; I knew it was coming.

Gregg Sarra asked, "Billy, how are you going to deal with the pressure as the season goes along?"

I responded with a prepared statement—I knew Gregg was a Pittsburgh Steelers fan, so I used a Chuck Noll saying, "Pressure is created by people who are not prepared. Hills West basketball will be prepared." The media loved it and gave us great reviews. It would be my job to keep the players away from the temptations that come with fame. That would be the hardest job, and it was an overwhelming task for myself and Bryan.

We started off with a slew of tough scrimmages in early December, including a trip upstate to last year's state champion Newburgh Free Academy, and hosting Rice HS of NYC. We played well because of our talent, but this was a new squad with a lot of big egos. I had to create a bond that would allow us to play well in big games, not just regular season games. The news media had us #1 in almost every poll across Long Island, but we had to prove ourselves to NYC and the country. So we put together a national schedule, playing teams like Bishop Loughlin of Brooklyn in the Big Apple Classic, a non-league game against Christ the King of Queens in Trenton, NJ, and traveling down to Morgantown, West Virginia to play the Pennsylvania state champion, Chester HS. We were invited to the Hoophall Classic in Springfield, Massachusetts to play the Connecticut state champ, Sacred Heart HS. This was going to be a lot of travelling, and a lot of time away from my wife and young children. This is something you can't prepare for, and again, you don't get paid extra for it. But it's a nice way to get exposure and national recognition for your players. Not bad for a coach who couldn't get his team in the playoffs four years ago. Basketball is a players' game, but good coaching is essential to a team's success.

Our first game was a league matchup at Eastport South Manor, which is an hour away on eastern Long Island. They were a solid team of lacrosse and football players, but didn't have much basketball talent. *Newsday* wrote an article promoting us, and 1,000 people showed up to watch us play. We put on a show in an easy win, but I didn't like what I was seeing. We weren't sharing the ball as I hoped, and our players weren't committing to our defense yet. But we had time to fix it before our first big games in mid-January against Sacred Heart and Bishop Loughlin.

Our season was broken down into three parts. The solid league season, the tough non-league games, and the playoffs. Our chemistry was not great yet; we needed a test to see how we would react under pressure. But our trip up to the Hoop Hall was very positive. On Martin Luther King Jr. weekend, we visited the Basketball Hall of Fame on Friday, defeated Sacred Heart of Connecticut on Saturday afternoon, and drove home that night. Most teachers have this weekend off, but I did not. We had to practice Sunday night in preparation for our big matchup with the #1 team in New York state, Bishop Loughlin.

We had a good practice on Sunday night, complete with a film session showing parts of the game we needed to improve on. I like to run the 1-3-1 three quarter court zone early in the season, because it teaches our players to help on defense and communicate. This would be our go-to defense if we got into foul trouble in NYC Monday night.

On Monday, we took the bus from Hills West at 4:30 to Baruch College in Manhattan for a 7 p.m. game. I scheduled this game first when Tobias came back to school because I'd gone to high school with its organizer, Jason Curry. We played in the Big Apple Classic two years ago and beat All Hallows. This game with Loughlin would answer three questions...

1. Could a Long Island team go into NYC and beat a Catholic League team?
2. Who was the best player in NYS? Tobias Harris or JayVaughn Pinkston?
3. Who was the best team in NYS?

This would be a monumental task, because we knew how good Loughlin was, but also playing in NYC would give us a disadvantage, being the road team. The game didn't start on time due to the long lineup of games that were played that day. MSG Network was broadcasting the game, and my old friend Mike Quick, who I met at Molloy in 1990, was covering the day of games. It was good to see him again, and a lot of my friends and colleagues came to support us. Baruch College was packed and the game started after 9.

In my coaching career, this was one of the most pressure-packed and fun games I've had the pleasure to coach. It was back and forth nonstop action. The crowd was on their feet, and both teams did not disappoint. Loughlin had a small lead in the first quarter until Tavon Sledge took over. We like to play a fast-paced style, and when the other team scores, we like to get the ball out and sprint. On a Loughlin made basket, Emile Blackman got the ball to Tavon, who took the ball the length of the court and hammered it over a Loughlin big man, which brought the capacity crowd to its feet. The two teams battled through halftime, but Pinkston gave Loughlin a small lead. Tobias was in foul trouble, so we had to hide him in the second half. We made an adjustment due to our foul trouble. We knew Loughlin didn't have great shooters, so we went to the 1-3-1 zone and it worked. Junior Anthony Rollino played well in the first half, so I put him in to play the zone, and he was awesome at sliding down and getting steals. Tobias took over the third quarter, and we took a twelve-point lead going into the fourth. Tyler Harris, Tavon Sledge, and Tobias Harris all hit big shots to get the lead to fifteen points, but we knew Loughlin would come back. With four minutes left in the game, up nine points, they called timeout, and I wanted to go back to man-to-man to finish strong. The guys wanted to stay in the 1-3-1, so I listened to them, since we were in foul trouble. Loughlin hit a quick three-pointer, and Tobias spoke to me in the huddle. "I'm sorry, Coach," he said with a smirk, "but don't worry, I got this. We're still going to win." We had a connection of trust, since I'd coached him for four years.

We went man-to-man on the next possession, and Loughlin got hot. With 28 seconds left and up two points, we got a big stop as Aaron McCree went to the line shooting two. Aaron hit the first to put us up three points, but missed the second. We actually got the offensive rebound, but lost it to Loughlin. With twelve seconds left, Loughlin missed a three-pointer to tie, but we didn't box out. The rebound came out to a Loughlin player, who passed it to JayVaughn Pinkston at the top of the key, and he nailed a three at the buzzer to put it into overtime. The crowd went into a frenzy, and I remember what I said to our guys in the huddle: "Hey! It's okay, we're going to win this game!" They looked at me with approval and believed me. That's why overtime went so well for us.

We hit our first shot, but so did Loughlin, and then Tobias fouled out of the game on a questionable offensive foul call. On the next play, Emile Blackman fouled out, and I grabbed a visibly upset Tobias

Harris and told him to be the biggest cheerleader and assistant coach right now. He did it right away.

We went down one point for the first time in three quarters, and Loughlin called timeout. I had a feeling they were going to press us full court, so I drew up our special press breaker play, called "Gold." They pressed us as expected, so we got the ball to Sledge sprinting full speed up the court, and he scored over their 6'9" center. We took the lead for good, and our 1-3-1 zone defense was the key. Tyler Harris and Anthony Rollino double-teamed Pinkston, and we sealed the game with great defense. Tavon got the winning rebound on the next possession, and we jumped up and down in a big celebration. MSG did a great job covering us, and now everyone knew we were a legitimate program.

Our Principal Deb Intorcia, Assistant Principal Frank Pugliese, and Athletic Director Joe Pennacchio were there to support us all season, and this night was no different. Deb grabbed me to congratulate me and said, "Bill, it's 11:00 p.m. right now. Most of the kids don't have a midterm tomorrow, so why don't you take your time coming in? Frank, make sure Bill has coverage for the morning so he can sleep in." You have no idea how important that one morning of sleep was to me. Deb, Frank, and Joe were all former coaches, and understood the commitment I had made to this team and our school. It's the little things sometimes that make you feel like a part of a team. I felt like I was appreciated by our administration in a year that was absolutely nonstop craziness. I'll never forget that small gesture she made on my behalf. There are very few people in society that think of others first before themselves. I was lucky to be surrounded by caring administrators early in my teaching career.

The rest of that season went as planned. We got to play a special non-league game before the playoffs in Trenton, NJ, against city powerhouse Christ the King. The same talented program from the late 1980s, but with a different coach. The new coach, Joe Arbitello, was introduced to me by Tom Konchalski. Tom is an outstanding human being and a wonderful talent evaluator. He came down to

Trenton to watch an entire day of basketball. I spoke with the coach of CTK, and he didn't know much about our team other than that we'd beaten Bishop Loughlin the month before. I wanted to beat them badly for what they'd done to us at Molloy my junior and senior years of high school. Our team played great and won a close game to go undefeated in the regular season. An added treat was that my father Angelo flew in from Vegas to watch us play the rest of the season. He got on the bus and sat with the team all the way to New Jersey. He had a wonderful talk with Tom Konchalski about 1950s basketball. I had a great day with Angelo, and now the playoffs were about to start.

My father did not want to miss the big games I coached in February and March. After my mother died of colon cancer in 2003, my father tried to make at least one trip to New York each year to spend time with the Mitaritonna family, mostly to take a break from the casinos of Las Vegas. My children loved having my father in town because that meant Dunkin Donuts every day. I loved having him at my games because he was a special set of eyes to watch my team at the end of our season. Angelo, the basketball coach, always picked up on the little things that you might miss after four months of coaching. For example, he picked up on the problem with Emile Blackman's foul shot. Angelo sat him down and told him to move his elbow in, so his ball would go straight in. Emile fixed it, and his foul shooting improved in the playoffs. My father had an eye for teaching great shooting form.

This was the second time in three years that we were listed as the one seed in the Suffolk County playoffs. We rolled through the first three games, and finally, the game everyone wanted to see was here: the Suffolk County Championship. The Longwood Lions were having a wonderful season as well, and we were matched up to play them for the county title at SUNY-Farmingdale. *Newsday* and *MSG Varsity* made a big deal out of the game, and 4,500 seats were filled, with about 500 people turned away. We were the favorite that everyone wanted to see lose, so Longwood had the underdog energy going into the game. They were without their point guard due to injury. We knew that feeling from two years ago, when we lost John Conneely to his appendectomy.

This game was as good as advertised. Longwood came out with energy and fire, and we matched them with our skill. Our game plan was to do what we'd done in every game this season: Pressure the other team with our help-side defense and overtake them in the fourth quarter. We were down one at the half, and we went into the locker room with optimism and positive thoughts. I went into the bathroom to use the facilities, and to my surprise, a father of one of my players tapped me on the shoulder and asked me why I wasn't playing a 2-3 zone defense! I was in shock, so all I said was, "Please get out of the locker room." But he continued to give me instructions. I just walked into the locker room and started talking to our guys, and my assistant coach Bryan Dugan escorted him out of the locker room with the help of a security guard. After we came back out onto the court for the second half, Coach Dugan and I got a good laugh out of that.

Tobias Harris got into foul trouble in the third quarter, so I sat him until the start of the fourth. Most coaches who have a player with four fouls in the third quarter will sit that player until four or five minutes or less are left. This is where having a relationship based on trust pays off. We went down three points to start the fourth quarter, and Tobias looked at me. I said, "Okay, get it done."

He said, "I'm going to win this game for you, Coach."

I replied very simply, "I believe you. Have fun."

We got a burst of energy from his return, and he didn't play like a man with four fouls. Tobias was our anchor on defense. Tavon Sledge stepped up in a big game again, and Emile Blackman kept us in it with his offensive rebounding and scoring. We were down 65-63 after a Longwood free throw with 3:30 left. We traded misses, and Tobias got a rebound and outletted the ball to Tavon, who brought it to the left side foul line extended. He caught Tobias trailing the play and passed him the ball above the three-point line. Tobias caught the ball in rhythm and took the shot. He nailed it: swish! The crowd went crazy, and Longwood called timeout.

This is when I appealed to my team's heart and courage. In the huddle, I told them this was where our defense worked best, and we should get together to finish them off. Up 66-65, we got the stop we needed, and Tavon brought the ball down the court. I made eye contact with Tyler Harris down the far sideline and called the play, "Baseline for Tyler," where he would use a baseline screen to take a three. His brother Tobias set a great screen, and Tyler hit the three right in front of our bench. I gave him a high five running back down the court, and we went up four points, 69-65. They called timeout again, and I told our guys to pressure them full court for the rest of the game. Two of their players cramped up on the court from our constant pressure. Tavon forced his man to throw an errant pass to Emile Blackman, who went to the basket to dunk the ball but was fouled. He hit one and we went up five points. I suddenly felt the weight of the world off my shoulders, because our game plan had worked. I was so happy for our guys because they believed in our plan. We finished strong on a 14-4 run, and Tobias came over to me as the clock ran down and said, "Coach, I told you I was going to win this game for you! Get over here, Coach!" We hugged at midcourt, and I thanked him for his efforts. The entire team was hugging each other and taking pictures to celebrate our second championship in three years. Our win earned the back page of *Newsday* the next morning, entitled "Hills Best."

After playoff games, we drive back with the team in the bus and talk about the upcoming schedule. The coaching staff and my colleagues at Hills West would always join me for a celebratory dinner afterwards. We were to meet at a local restaurant, but as I got into my car to leave school, a father of one of my players cornered me in the parking lot. He started yelling at me because his son didn't play a lot in this game. We'd won one of the most attended games in Suffolk County history, I hadn't been home in four months, it was almost midnight, and this man decided this was a good time to tell me how bad a coach I was. Due to playing time, which happens to be the number one complaint I received from parents in my coaching career. This should have been a fun night for me, my family, and the Hills West community. Yet two parents could not handle themselves in a big moment, and I was not able to fully enjoy this win.

The following week, we defeated Uniondale High School at Hofstra University in the Long Island Championship to earn a berth to the semifinals of the state tournament. This was a crazy week, to say the least. Dealing with the media coverage alone was an ordeal. I had newspaper, websites, and cable TV calling all week long, on top of teaching my classes. And of course, trying to be a father to my children and husband to my wife. Since Tobias came back to school eleven months earlier in April, my job was to stay in contact with colleges for him: writing recommendations for player of the year, handling media requests, and keeping up constant contact with his father, as well as taking care of my teaching responsibilities. What the general public does not see on the outside is the stress this took on myself and my family. From September to late March, I was an absentee father and husband. Taking phone calls at home from parents at the dinner table was annoying. Getting negative emails from parents on Christmas Day. Not being able to sleep because I was watching film or creating a practice plan until 1:00 a.m., and then getting up at 6:00 to teach five classes. Maybe grab a nap for ten minutes, run a two to three-hour practice, and repeat daily. This routine for five months takes a toll on a person.

Why do people like myself do it? It's not for the money, that's for sure. If you divide the number of hours by the actual salary, it works out to less than $1.00 per hour. You have no time to work out and take care of your body because you're eating fast food on the way home from practice. Overall, it's not the healthiest of lifestyles, but I never coached for the money, awards, or publicity. I did it for the same reason my father did. He always loved to look at the smiling faces after a win or a season. Angelo talked of the feeling you get from working together to achieve a goal. Coach Graffam gave me the tools to make that happen. I did it for the gratification you get when you work together to achieve a goal as a unit. I find it unfair that high school coaches are criticized as much as college or pro coaches who make millions. On the most basic level, we're teachers. Working with teenagers is hard to begin with. Add in academic pressures, getting into college, social media, dating, work, families, and friends. Then we have to get a group of individuals to buy into the system to create a team. The constant distractions behind the scenes are always there to put doubt into the minds of your players. What do parents want high school coaches to do? Again, no money, time away from your family, and not taking care of your health, all for an unknown. We don't know how a season will end up. We might have an expectation to do well, but there are no guarantees when coaching young people. And we're teaching life lessons, using the sport we coach. That's how I was brought up, and that's how I will continue to coach my children. Coach Graffam always spoke of "doing the right thing." That is exactly what I have done in my coaching career.

We went upstate to Glens Falls, NY for the state tournament, and I was exhausted. The entire week was overwhelming, and it was just my assistant coach and myself to take care of all the responsibilities to play in the final four. We arrived to Glens Falls and had a team shootaround at a local high school, then talked about our eating schedule and nighttime hotel procedures.

On Saturday, we played a very tough Rochester East team, and Tobias hit a shot with five seconds left to win the game for us. It was the closest game all season. After the game, Tobias was presented with two awards: He was selected the New York Sportswriters Player of the Year, and Gatorade Player of the Year for New York State. He was well deserving of both, and we found out later on in the week of a third selection. Tobias would be representing the East squad and playing in the McDonald's All-American Game in late March. What a month for a great kid.

We had a large crowd that travelled upstate, complete with my wife and three children. Ernie and Walter drove up to see us. They were a part of my summer softball team, and two of the reasons why I got into games at St. John's in 1993. They were two of my biggest fans, and I always appreciated their support. My father was in New York for my 2008 championship, but stayed in Las Vegas for most of this basketball season. He went back to Vegas after the county final, so I would call him after every playoff game to give him updates. Luckily, a lot of our games were streamed live on *MSG Varsity*, so he could watch our games from his home in Vegas.

The state championship was played on a Sunday, but the perfect storm happened, and we were on the wrong side of it. The crowd was big for Christian Brothers Academy of Albany, which was 45 minutes away. Our team was tense and feeling the pressure of winning 25 straight games. We lost miserably, and the game felt like it lasted forever. But there was one bright spot. Junior Tavon Sledge scored 35 points, and willed our team back into the game almost by himself. Every time he got the ball in transition, he was able to get to the basket and either score or get fouled. Tavon has the heart of a lion and the motor to back it up. I was proud of our team nonetheless. After the game, our guys were distraught, and the bus ride home was even worse. This season made me think about how much I needed to take care of my family and myself.

The next day, I walked into the athletic director's office and resigned due to the pressures of coaching a nationally ranked team and the need to spend more time with my wife and kids. To my athletic director's credit, Joe Pennacchio refused to take the resignation and told me to go on vacation with my family. We would talk again in the spring. He knew how much time and effort I put into the season, and the toll it took on my well-being. I needed a big-time break. The next two months were very restful, and I got a chance to reconnect with my family and friends. My returning players pushed me to return next year, especially Emile Blackman, Chris Cox, and Tavon Sledge. I absolutely loved and respected these kids, so I returned as head coach for 2011.

CHAPTER TWENTY-TWO

A REWARDING SEASON

THE 2010-2011 SCHOOL year was one of my favorites from start to finish. In the fall, we had a great start to the school year. Homecoming week was outstanding. One of my many duties at Hills West was to MC the pep rally the night before the Homecoming parade and football game. This pep rally would go down as the best in school history. The class of 2011 had great energy and so much school spirit. They were known as "wild" but I loved them. They had a great example set in the graduating class of 2008 three years before, and I taught four 12th-grade government classes, so we had a great relationship.

In November, as the season started, I pushed the theme of "Together" more than any other season since my first year coaching in 2000. I had a great core of seniors who had played together two years ago before Tobias Harris transferred back to Hills West. Seniors Chris Cox, Chris Kaimis, Anthony Rollino, and Tavon Sledge, as well as Junior Emile Blackman, all had at least a year of varsity playing experience to draw from. I have learned over time that if you have seniors with experience, your team will be hard to beat. Not only did we have experience, but we had courage and talent. I always remember what the coaches from Idaho taught me years ago. You need kids that compete every day in practice and refuse to lose. And I knew we had that in the 2011 squad. Chris Kaimis was the best volleyball player on Long Island, and had already won four Long Island championships in two sports. Anthony Rollino was a fearless pass-first player, and a superior defensive presence at point guard. Chris Cox was our most improved player, with outstanding athletic ability. Emile Blackman was a future college basketball player who was the best dunker in New York state. And Tavon Sledge was a future Division One player and a winner, period. Losing was not in his emotional or physical makeup. These five players had the makings of a championship team.

Due to our national non-league schedule, we did not start until January 3rd. We scrimmaged as many teams as I could find, but sometimes that's how your schedule works out. I really pushed them mentally and physically through the month of December. They were sick of the scrimmages and ready to compete. As always, I wasn't happy with our team defense. It traditionally clicks in mid to late-January. When you coach a team of successful and talented kids, you have to manage egos and create a bond that will carry them for the season. But it was easy for me to manage the egos, because the players weren't happy about how last season had ended. They were driven to repeat as champions.

My motto for this year was "Together" as always, but I started to talk about what we could do "Today" to get better as a team. As a social studies teacher, I study important people in history. Mother Teresa said, "Yesterday is gone. Tomorrow has not yet come. We have only today. Let us begin." I took that saying from 2007-08 and geared it towards my team. I began the season by saying we should "Control Today" and used it each day in practice. Kids today have so many distractions, and it can be hard to keep them focused, so I wanted them to practice mental as well as physical abilities. It turned into something I use today in life with my own children. It evolved into, "Control today, guys, yesterday is over and tomorrow is not a guarantee." I pounded that into their minds, and it became very useful later in the season for a lot of reasons. I also made an addition to my coaching staff. Steve Atkinson was a friend and former championship coach at Hauppauge HS. He was so excited to join the staff, and he was invaluable scouting and helping us in practice. More importantly, the players absolutely loved his positive attitude towards life.

We were invited to go upstate to play in a Hoop Group event at Skidmore College against Albany Academy. Sledge and Emile led us in scoring, and we had a long trip home. This was another example of leaving my family on a Sunday early in the morning and getting home late at night. On that bus ride home, I made a point to go and speak to all ten guys coming off the bench to get to know them. Coaching the kids on the bench is always a lot harder than coaching the starters. I'd carefully selected my bench for this year. Our bench was going to be important in preparing our starters every day, and they had to be great kids: solid citizens who were respected by our staff and student body. We ended up with a nice mix of seniors and underclassmen. Our first league game was against Deer Park on the road two days later, and they were not able to scout us because we hadn't played any games on Long Island. We won a close game, and we were starting to play as a unit.

The following Saturday afternoon, we had a game set up with Archbishop Molloy and Coach Curran. We had played a couple of times in the past, but this was going to be a great test for our guys. It was always fun to go back and see Coach Curran, Fran Leary, and my former teachers. Coach Curran did something for me every time I played there. He came into the gym and sat with me for twenty minutes (the entire warm-up) to talk basketball. He NEVER did that for other coaches. Coach would usually come out with four minutes in the warm-up. On this day, we had an awesome conversation about high school basketball. He mentioned to me that his current team had talent, but they wouldn't listen to him. Coach also spoke of parents who were on his back. I couldn't believe parents were criticizing Coach Curran, who had won 900 basketball games in 53 seasons. I was very upset by that. He was so important to so many kids over the years, and he didn't deserve that disrespect.

The game was back and forth, and a lot of fun to watch. Again, I didn't like our defense, and our shot selection looked like a bad AAU game. We were dribbling too much and taking too many three-pointers. The game was filled with dunks by Emile, Tavon, and Chris, and filmed by *MSG Varsity*. The game came down to the end, and we were up two points as Emile Blackman stepped up to the foul line for an and-one with five seconds left. Coach Curran called timeout, and I made a mistake in the huddle. I assumed Emile would hit both and we would win. I never told the team what to do if he missed. Obviously, our guys should know how to react in an end of game situation, but as a coach, you need to cover it, because they're teenagers. Emile went to the line and missed, a Molloy player rebounded the ball, dribbled three times, and put up a shot right over half court. SWISH! Their team celebrated, and Coach Curran started walking toward me with a big smile and his deep-sounding signature laugh: "Huh huh huh! Great game, Billy. That kid Sledge is wonderful. Good luck this season." It was a vintage, old-school win in his gym with his name on the court. My guys were upset, and Emile was sad because he wanted to win for me. I told him that was nice, but not our reason for competing every day. Up next was a big league game on Tuesday at West Babylon.

We had a good practice on Monday, but our defense and shot selection were not where I wanted them to be, as usual. Tuesday's game at West Babylon caught me and our guys off guard. Their team was on fire, they had a great game plan, and their crowd was the best we had seen in years. They took it to us and played great, but we helped them out by taking 27 quick, poor shots and making 14 turnovers. In my mind, taking a poor shot led to easy offense for the other team. I was steaming after the game, because we preach "Together," and our guys were very overconfident from reading our press clippings. We played selfish and gave up 81 points, a lot more than our goal of giving up 45 PPG.

That night was a long one for me. I got home at 9:30 p.m. after picking up Wendy's burgers and started to break down the film. I watched the film once without stopping it to pick up on trends, and then again to track certain stats. By the time I was finished, it was 1:30 a.m., and I had to get up for school at 6:00. The next day in school, the team completely ducked me in the hallway. They knew that their performance was not up to Hills West standards, and Wednesday afternoon's film session was brutal. I took the five starters aside and slammed them for a lack of togetherness, awful shot selection, and horrendous defense. I put up their stats on my classroom board and told them, "The film don't lie, boys." We spent two hours in the classroom breaking down each possession. Our shooting percentage was under 20%, and giving up 81 points was against everything I believed in as a defensive coach. This film session was a turning point in our season, and I made a switch at the guard position. I put Tavon Sledge at the shooting guard and moved Anthony Rollino to his natural point guard spot. The results were instantaneous. Two days after the West Babylon game, we had a big home game against Bellport. Our defense was the key, and the players were starting to trust each other. Anthony got the ball to the right person, and Sledge had 35 points, letting the game come to him. We were slowly starting to get it, but we still had some things to fix.

After three weeks of league wins, the rematch with West Babylon was coming to Hills West in early February. *MSG Varsity* was coming to televise the game, and our gym was packed once again, like last year. West Babylon brought a big crew of students to cheer, and this game was for first place. An hour and a half before the game, I asked the five starters into the guidance office conference room and we sat down to talk. They looked very nervous to be in this room with me. I'd been really rough on them in practice over the last three weeks, and rightfully so, because they'd been very selfish.

I started my talk with, "Guys, you are the reason why I came back to coach this year. Yes, I was disappointed after the first West Babylon game. But today, I wanted to bring you in to let you know how proud I am of your progress." The nervous looks on their faces turned into smiles. I let the 2010-11 squad know they were capable of going upstate and winning. They needed to know that I was proud of their improvement. This was a big game, and our guys were fired up leaving that office. In later years, Chris Cox mentioned to me that this moment created our family bond, and we felt unstoppable as a unit.

West Babylon had a great team that year with a lot of talent, but our five starters were not going to let them breathe for a second without being smothered on defense. We got out to a 10-0 lead behind six quick points by Chris Cox. Chris was without question our most improved player from two years ago. He was now able to get to the basket and dunk in traffic. Chris could shoot the outside jumper, and more importantly, had the confidence to do anything he wanted on the court. He helped us get a quick lead, but in the second quarter, Emile Blackman did something I've never seen before and probably will never see again. Up 14 points, we ran a play called "Duke" where a high screen and roll was run by Anthony Rollino for our backup center, Neneyo Mate-Kole. The ball was passed to Neneyo, but ricocheted into the hands of Emile, who leaped off two feet from under the basket and dunked it with authority. Our fans started to heat up, and on the next play, West Babylon missed a shot, we brought the ball down, and Chris Kaimis took a three-pointer from the right side. The ball rebounded long, into the right hand of Emile Blackman, who hammered it down again for an emphatic slam. The place went crazy, and our guys "smelled blood." In other words, be a shark, smell the blood, and attack. Anthony Rollino smelled it, made a spectacular hustle play at half court on the next possession to steal the ball, dove on the floor, and had the guts to pass it to Emile, who tomahawked *another* dunk and sent our crowd into a frenzy. In that timeout by our opponent, I didn't have to say a word. Carl Reuter and Rob Pavinelli of *MSG Varsity* noted that three dunks in 90 seconds had to be a record, and Carl noted, "All due respect to Emile's uncle Mark Jackson, but Mark could never do what Emile just did." He was right. We were up 19 at the half, but I didn't want us to stop. We continued the pressure, and Chris Cox started the half with two spectacular dunks of his own and had a career high of 19 points to lead us. We held them to 42 points (down from 81 points three weeks ago) and we were now "Together." We ended up tied for first place in the league, and captured the one seed in the playoffs for the third time in four years.

There was one game at the end of that season that stuck out for our program. We travelled to Comsewogue High School in Port Jefferson Station to finish the regular season, against a team who had not won a game all year. It was Valentine's Day, and as we entered the gym to watch the JV game, we found a larger crowd than usual. That instantly caught my attention. We always came out here for games, and it would normally be filled with parents and maybe a couple of students. Coming up from the locker room to warm up, we could hear the Comsewogue student section start to cheer. My assistant coach Steve Atkinson grabbed me and said, "Coach, these kids are here to see us play. I asked a supervisor and she said the kids watched our dunks against West Babylon on MSG and they were impressed!"

I looked at him and smiled. "Are you kidding me?"

Coach Atkinson replied with a smile as well. "Coach, we're big time!" Then he laughed sarcastically.

We got into the huddle, and I used the crowd noise to my advantage. I told our kids that Comsewogue was here to knock us out of the top seed in the playoffs and win their last home game on senior night. Our team bought it and went out with a laser focus. That lasted two minutes, as Chris Cox stole a pass and dunked the ball on a fast break. The crowd erupted and started to put up pieces of paper with the numbers 9 and 10 on them, like the NBA dunk contest. Emile picked up on it first and yelled to me during a foul shot, "They're here for us!" The bench got fired up because we had eight or nine players that could dunk. We kept our constant pressure on and got steal after steal, but the other team refused to let us dunk. Comsewogue got upset that their own student body was cheering for Hills West. I got our team together after the first quarter and told them to get a nice lead so I could take out my starters. I didn't want a turned ankle right before the playoffs. Tavon, Emile, and Chris caught some nice dunks, and notably, Emile threw an alley-oop to Tavon for a crowd-pleasing slam. We broke the game open, everyone played, and we got on the bus to ride home. Our program had now risen to a level I hadn't seen since the Kenny Anderson Molloy teams of the 1980s.

We won our first two playoff games easily, and had six days to prepare for the semifinals at Stony Brook. That's when tragedy struck. This is where my "control today" phrase came into play on a personal level. During the February winter break, Emile and Jamir Blackman's Uncle Troy, aka "Escalade" Jackson, passed away at an early age. He was an amazing young man. They were obviously devastated, and Emile needed to get out of the house. I drove out the day after it happened and took him and his brother to practice, so they could get their grief out by playing basketball. The team showed up and we practiced with heavy hearts. Troy was our biggest fan and a great guy. He was also Emile's male influence and role model in life. Troy had always been there for Emile. This was heartbreaking to watch. But Emile played on another level that day, and our guys couldn't stop him. I had never seen this side of him; he was definitely in the zone.

After practice, Emile came with me to lunch and we talked about how bad today would be, as well as the next month or so. We spoke about how Emile had to be strong for his mother Ana and his grand-mother Marie. He was still in shock, and I told him that I would pick him up anytime he needed a ride or to talk. Our team was visibly upset, and I had to handle this over February break when school was closed. That was not an easy week.

The funeral was set for the following Tuesday, the same day as the semifinal game. There was no discussion of Emile missing the game. Troy would want him to play and win. The funeral was a big reception of people celebrating Troy's life at the Upper Room Tabernacle in Dix Hills. It was a long day, and our guys were emotionally exhausted. Emile, Jamir, and Tavon were hit very hard by Troy's death, so I let them come with their families to Stony Brook to spend time at the funeral. We played that night in the second of two games, and defeated William Floyd in a close matchup. We walked into the locker room, and the team was beyond tired, emotionally and physically. I told them that we'd be off tomorrow and practice on Thursday. Our county championship matchup was Friday night at Stony Brook against West Babylon.

A lot of players spent time in guidance, speaking with counselors on Wednesday and Thursday, and rightfully so. Troy was so close to our program and a larger-than-life figure. Thursday's practice was thirty minutes of film and thirty minutes of shooting. Our starters had no legs and we were emotionally exhausted. My assistant coaches felt it was important to take it easy and save it for the game. They were right.

But when Friday night came, we looked exhausted again on the bus. I couldn't really blame them, and I basically said to them, "Guys, I love you all, so go out and do this for Troy. He was at every big game, so get it done for him, but more importantly, each other." They looked at each other, and sadness turned to focus. We played inspired basketball, but West Babylon was tough, and we won by eight points. Usually, when a team wins a county championship, a group of young men will celebrate by jumping up and down, screaming, etc. Our guys didn't do that. Other than a couple of hugs, we shook the other team's hands and walked into the locker room. No fanfare, no one was out of control. The entire team was in tears, and we took our time to get home. I was so proud of them to step up and get it done under these circumstances.

A leader will sometimes have to make unpopular decisions at the time to do what's right. This was the case two days later after our county win. I called our five starters on Saturday afternoon to see how they were feeling. We had a game scheduled on Sunday morning by Section XI to see who the best team in Suffolk was, a game that had no bearing on whether we were playing in the Long Island Championship. We were playing Elmont next Sunday at Stony Brook no matter what. So I made the decision to sit my starters in the game on Sunday, because they were absolutely exhausted. I didn't want anyone to get hurt, and I was the only person who knew how emotionally tired they were, especially Tavon and Emile. When we came out of the locker room, people saw our starters in street clothes and started to yell and curse me out from the stands. The media and reporters wanted an explanation, and Suffolk County was upset. People were planning to see us play Harborfields, whom we'd beaten last year in this same game without Tobias Harris playing, so what was the big deal? Gregg Popovich, the head coach of the San Antonio Spurs, had been criticized for doing this with Tim Duncan earlier in the year. They tried to compare the two in the newspaper and on the Internet.

But in my heart, I knew this was the best thing for my team. Our guys were still hurting from last week, and I was their coach. It's my job, and my job alone, to determine the starting lineup for any game. We played our bench and they appreciated the experience. Kids that hadn't played the entire season got a chance to play in front of a big crowd. The game ended, we lost, and I was surrounded by the media and reporters. To this day, I have no idea why this was such a big deal. No one has the right to criticize me but me. Teddy Roosevelt said that 100 years ago: the credit goes to the man in the arena, not the people on the sidelines. My players really respected me for it, and at the end of the day, that's the only thing I really care about. That went a long way in helping out after a tough week.

We had a great week of practice in preparing for the Long Island Championship on Sunday. I gave the kids Monday and Tuesday off to rest up and come back fresh. We sat down as a team on Wednesday and spoke about the rest of the week leading up to Sunday afternoon. Dad flew in from Las Vegas to spend time with family in Suffolk County, so it would be a quick commute to Stony Brook University for him. For some reason, I felt very comfortable coaching at Stony Brook. I can't put my finger on why, but I'd never lost an elimination game in that arena. There are some places in life that make you feel at home. I feel at home in my classroom, I feel at home in a gym while I coach basketball, I feel at home every time I drive over the Cross Bay Bridge into Rockaway Beach, I feel at home while being with my family in the Bahamas, and I feel at home walking the sideline at Stony Brook University.

Our game was to start at 3:30 p.m. on Sunday afternoon against Nassau County Champion Elmont HS. They'd beaten Baldwin 32-29 the week before, and I told our guys that the score didn't indicate how physical and athletic they could be. We needed to be ready, physically and emotionally. Most people had us as the favorite, because we were playing at home in Suffolk County, we were defending champs, and we had Tavon Sledge. Tavon had been playing at a high level the last two months, and when the lights went on, he stepped up his game. In my eighteen years of coaching high school basketball, I had some great competitors, but no one could top Sledge. He was First Team All-State and Player of the Year on Long Island, and about to set a record in this game that might never be beaten.

Our Long Island Championship win last year over Uniondale had been uneventful. We won by fifteen points in a so-so game. This matchup with Elmont was the opposite. It had pure drama, due to the athleticism of both squads, explosive scorers, and fast-paced basketball. I walked into the locker room before the game, and the kids were very reserved and focused. All five of our starters had played in the state tournament last year, so this game wasn't going to make them nervous. I read their faces and told them to go out and have fun. They deserved to play in this game, so why not enjoy it? It's high school basketball, it's supposed to be fun. The entire team smiled, and our captains brought us in close for our routine pregame chant of "Together!"

My philosophy on in-game coaching is simple. Criticize and coach them in practice, make adjustments and cheer for them in games. It's too late to teach them new plays, too late to put in a new defense, too late to put in a player who hasn't played all playoffs. My five starters were getting the opportunity to win another Long Island Championship they so deserved.

The game went back and forth, with leads exchanged each passing minute. Both teams played at a high level during regulation. The game with Elmont went to overtime, as they hit a layup at the buzzer to send the crowd into a frenzy. They took the lead on a layup with less than a minute remaining in the first overtime, and Sledge, who had 37 points at this point, took the ball to the basket. It seemed everything he put up was going in, but this time he lost the ball, and Elmont stole it for a layup going the other way. Their crowd went absolutely berserk. This was devastating. For the only time in the game, I had a quick feeling of losing. All the free throws we missed, all the turnovers, all the time I put into working with this group, it could possibly end...and then I remembered Sledge was wearing a Superman costume under his Hills West uniform.

It's weird what you see as a coach from the sideline during a big moment. As we brought the ball up the court, losing by three points with twenty seconds left, I made eye contact with Chris Cox, and he had a look of devastation on his face. He looked at me and tilted his head down, as if we'd lost. It only took two seconds, and I yelled out play "1" for Sledge. The play that had never worked in any game. The play I'd put in three weeks ago from Tom Izzo. We ran it to perfection, and Sledge came around the last screen up top from Chris Kaimis. His footwork was perfect, his shooting form was solid, and he took an NBA-type three-pointer with an Elmont player in his face. The ball left his hands, and the entire crowd gasped. The ball had a rainbow arc on it; it felt like it was in the air for ten seconds. My reaction before his shot was stoic, and it didn't change after the ball gently dropped through the rim. Our bench celebrated, along with the Hills West faithful, as Elmont grabbed the ball for one last shot, but it had no chance of going in. We knew we were going to double overtime and had momentum.

The buzzer sounded, and Sledge walked off the court with no emotion on his face. He looked possessed. I let the guys sit and get a drink while I conferred with my assistants. This was a different huddle than after the game had ended in regulation. As the starting five walked out to play the second overtime, Sledge grabbed me and brought me in close so no one else could hear. He said, "I'm going to win this game for you, Coach. I'm going to win this game for us."

I said very simply, "I believe you. Have fun."

He walked away, and I knew we were going to win. No matter what, Sledge was going to get this done. Tavon was a winner in life. He had been through a lot in his short life, and he always had a way of landing on his feet.

In the second overtime, I sat down in a relaxed position for almost the entire period. After some time sitting down, Andrew Rappaport of *News 12 Sports* asked me a question from the scorer's table.

"Coach, you look pretty relaxed for the second overtime of the Long Island Championship game."

I smiled at him and said, "Do you see number three in white? He's on my team. We'll be just fine in his hands."

Tavon took the game over by determination and will. Elmont called timeout with .8 seconds left while we were up three points, so I brought the entire team together to tell them something important. I instructed them to not celebrate after the game. We were to shake the other team's hands and walk back to the bench. Sledge hit the last free throw to end the game, and our players followed my instructions perfectly. We hugged briefly and did the right thing. The *MSG Varsity* announcers, Carl Reuter and Rob Pavinelli, commented that we didn't celebrate out of respect for Elmont. They were right on the money. Elmont had played an outstanding game, in what the media called an instant classic. Tavon finished with 46 points, which is still a Long Island playoff record today. He didn't care if it was 6 points or 46 points, he just wanted to get this win for us. After the game, he was interviewed by Rob Pavinelli about why he'd played so well. Tavon replied, "I told my coach I was going to win this game for him, and that's what I did. I wasn't losing this game."

What an amazing young man. Tavon will always go down as an all-time winner in Hills West Basketball, and Long Island basketball history. I was asked by a reporter if sitting my five starters last week in the overall Section XI game was the right move, since we won in double overtime. I responded with, "I'm not going to comment on that, but what do you think?" and we both laughed. In my mind, I was so happy that good things happen to good people. Again, that's what my parents always said.

We absolutely enjoyed the next week at school and left for Glens Falls on Friday morning. We were matched up with Mount Vernon, the number one team in the state, who had combo guard Jabarie Hinds, one of the top players in the state. Jabarie had a strong physique and a plethora of offensive skills. He was committed to West Virginia for a reason. Mount Vernon was no stranger to this tournament, after winning several state titles over the last fifteen years, but we had an advantage. Tavon had grown up playing against Jabarie and had great success guarding him; he always locked him up. It was hard to scout teams from out of Long Island. We did our best to get reports on them, but our guys were so confident it didn't matter. We had a great dinner Friday night and woke up the next morning to beautiful late March temperatures. Our game started at 1:15, and we were so excited. The atmosphere with our team was so different this time around. Our guys were truly together. All five starters had played in this arena before, so we had another advantage. The game was like any other game we had played in the playoffs. Up a few points, down a few points, and Sledge was locking up Hinds. He couldn't breathe. Hinds got in foul trouble, so we now had to take advantage. What we didn't know was how deep Mount Vernon was on the bench. They had 6'4" junior guard Isaiah Cousins, who eventually played for Oklahoma, come off the bench, and he scorched us. Sledge ended up with 18 points, while Hinds finished with 10. Emile Blackman had a game-high 25, and Chris Cox had some high-flying dunks, but Mount Vernon was too deep and we lost by four points. That was a tough game to swallow, because we were tied with three minutes left. They ended up winning the NY State and Federation titles. Sledge bent down to his knees, and I picked him up off the floor. He put his head into my chest, and I told him that he'd had a wonderful high school basketball career at Hills West, but this was not the end for him.

CHAPTER TWENTY-THREE

SCRATCHING THE ITCH

BY 2014, after some very good seasons record-wise, we hadn't won a championship since 2011. I enjoyed coaching some wonderful young men who graduated in those years, but we never got out of the second round of the playoffs. My wife and kids were always there to pick up the pieces for me emotionally after each season. It was hard for me to not get to the finals and compete for a championship. When we won three championships in four years, I got used to that winning feeling, but three seasons of not getting there made me want to work harder. Billy Donovan, former University of Florida head coach and current NBA head coach for the Oklahoma City Thunder, said, "As a coach, I had winning seasons and losing seasons, but my mindset changed over time. I used to judge my success on results, but now my mindset is based on if I made a difference in a player's life. How will players talk about me in the future? How will they tell their children about me? That will be my legacy as a coach." This is a man who won back-to-back NCAA Championships in 2006 and 2007 at the University of Florida, and he wasn't concerned with wins and losses anymore. That made an impression on me, and I started to concentrate on the process and journey more than my winning percentage. The reality of coaching a high school sport is treating your players well and making sure they have fun. I could honestly look back at my coaching career and say without a doubt, our teams always had fun. So I asked my former players to come to our games during the 2014-15 and 2015-16 seasons and talk to our players about their Hills West basketball experience. It worked so well, because I found out how many guys loved playing high school basketball for me. In the end, that's worth more to me than money or winning championships.

We got to the Suffolk County Championship game in 2015, but lost to Brentwood by 20 points. The 2014-2015 Colts were resilient, and they overachieved. We didn't expect to get so far. Our team was a mix of solid veterans and my youth movement: Sophomore Cameron Jordan and Juniors Deven Williams, Kian Dalyrimple, and Richard Altenord. We finished with a 19-3 record, and I was very happy with our improvement throughout the year. We had some highlights that are worth noting, too. We got to the final four and played Copiague for the third time in one season. The head coach of Copiague is Steve Rebholz, a wonderful teacher who won back-to-back championships in 2006 and 2007. In all three games with Copiague, we were losing in the second half by double digits, but came back to win, including a final four game at SUNY-Farmingdale. It showed our team could take a hit and keep moving forward. I liked our chances for the next season with our varsity experience. This "Core Four" had what it takes to take the next step.

After the season ended, I was able to find another video of Billy Donovan speaking about championship teams. Coach Donovan outlined what all successful teams have in common. A love for each other, care for each other, and acceptance for everyone on the roster. Our 2014-15 team had those three components, and our team coming back was no different. They deeply cared about each other, and it was a good mix of personalities. During the 2015-16 high school basketball season, we had a talented group who had outstanding chemistry and passion. I worked with this unit for three long years where we took our lumps. The "Core Four" were best friends off the court, and it made them much easier to coach. At the same time, I've never felt more on top of my coaching game.

Every year that I coached high school basketball, I learned so much from observing other coaches, watching old game film from past seasons, and learning from my students and assistant coaches. This season was different, because I was equipped to give us every opportunity to be successful by purchasing the online film service HUDL. It allowed me to get film on every team we faced, and I spent countless hours breaking down our team and opponents. I finally understood what my good friend Kyle Madden, the Hills West football coach, meant about the importance of film study. Not from the standpoint of players watching film, like we did at St. John's, but more for myself and my assistant coach Steve Atkinson. After losing badly to Brentwood the year before in the Suffolk County Championship, we watched a lot of film to get ready for the season.

The entire team had a bad taste in their mouth, so we were collectively determined to "Get it Done" this season. I wanted to give our team every advantage.

The basketball season started slow, because we had to wait for our All-County football player, junior wide receiver, and power forward Cameron Jordan to finish his football season. He was playing in the Suffolk County football championship game for Hills West. Our goals were simple and had been for the last ten years: get in shape, control today, and do it together. Each of those three goals had a specific meaning to our players that was very important to our team's success.

Getting in shape is vital to our team philosophy of playing great help-side defense and running the fast break. We proved in 2007-08 with our first championship that it works great if all players understand and accept our system. Like 2007-08, the 2015-16 squad had the pieces in place to make another run. Coach Graffam always said getting in shape is a part of the game that you can control, and when other teams are fading at the end of the game, the better-conditioned team will have a big advantage. This would be the difference in close games. After committing to our help-side defense and fast break system in 2005-06, we never missed the playoffs and won 76% of our games overall. (81% since the start of 2009-10.) How did we start each season? Conditioning stations, just like we did at Westbrook College with Coach Graffam. Our conditioning stations achieved several goals for us all in one week. The boys would each have to complete athletic tasks during the five days while depending on each other. Every player would rely on each other to get the running done in under a specific time. By listing specific times to beat, the players got better each day and had a sense of accomplishment. Basketball is a game of beating the clock as well as beating your opponent. Our conditioning stations achieved both at the same time. I became the facilitator and watched our players become a team.

The 2015-16 Hills West squad had speed, athleticism, high basketball IQ, and unselfishness. Any championship team must be unselfish throughout the season in order to be successful. Along with talent, a team needs to buy into a philosophy. It's a coach's responsibility to have everyone believe in a philosophy that all players and parents can understand. I started the theme of "Together" in 2000, because it was something that bonded us as a program immediately. Over the years, the theme of "Together" took on a life of its own. Players from all different backgrounds became family through our program, something I could not have envisioned when I took over. As years went by, I wanted to help these high school teenagers focus. So I continued to use, "Yesterday is over, tomorrow is not a guarantee, Control Today." I started using it in 2008 for our first championship team with great success. I wanted to help our players focus on the practice, or the game, and nothing else. That also meant, if we had a bad day yesterday, forget about it and move on. And lastly, don't talk about anything regarding the future, because too many things can change daily. My goal was to give my players a philosophy they could grasp and believe in, since I feel that too many high school coaches don't have a philosophy that teenagers can believe in and implement. It took me years as a varsity coach to figure out what works and then be able to put it into action on the high school level. Our philosophy works because our players believe in their coaches.

There was something special about this group of young men: junior forward Cameron Jordan, Senior point guard Deven Williams, Senior shooting guard Kian Dalyrimple, and Senior guard/wing Richard Altenord. I was very particular about who I would put on the team to surround the core four. They had to be unselfish and willing to accept a limited role. I learned at St. John's how damaging "the disease of me" could be to a team. We had a junior guard transfer in named Matthew Asenjo who needed to learn how to play varsity basketball, but he had skill and potential. We rounded out the eight-man rotation with three physical athletes to give us depth.

Going back to the importance of film. HUDL allowed us to get film on our long-time league rival, Deer Park. They would be an early challenge for us, so I called a friend who'd played them the week before to watch film so I could get a feel for their personnel and tendencies. It was a tremendous help. My assistant coach, Steve Atkinson, and myself, sat and watched it for hours, over and over again for three days. After analyzing it, we used six clips of film. We showed the team very little for a reason. Teenagers have a short attention span. I have showed too much film in the past, and it has backfired. During the early days of my coaching career, I thought showing the entire game to the players would help, but it was counterproductive. So we designed a game plan, double-teaming their best player every time he used a high ball screen. He would have to pass to someone else and they would shoot. Our game plan was to defend, rebound, and run, and that's what we did for four quarters. It was so important to get a league win early in the season.

That win would be the start of four tough games in our schedule. Non-league games are scheduled early in the season so you can film them and get better as a team. We played in the very popular Baldwin Tournament for the second straight year, and led off against the Catholic school power Holy Trinity. The fans that showed up for our game over the Christmas break were treated to an offensive shootout. I was very happy with our ability to compete against an excellent team. Both teams went back and forth trading baskets, but we pulled away in the end, and our conditioning was the difference. We were able to make a run in the fourth quarter to seal the win. Kian Dalyrimple was our leading scorer, but I didn't like how he was playing. He was a remarkable shooter and scorer, but his help defense was not where I wanted it to be, and he was still dribbling too much. Kian was in his own world at times, and his own friends saw it, but I'm very good in situations like this with players who aren't buying into our system. We played Baldwin the next night in the championship game, and they've always been a pain in my side. Coach Darius Burton is an excellent and very passionate teacher. (He also covered me so tight at St. John's while playing for Hofstra that I couldn't get a shot off back in 1993.) We played very well in this game, but fell apart in the third quarter. I did something in this game that I rarely do: get a technical foul. I only get a tech when I want to change the momentum of the game or fire up my players. So I decided to choose a referee I knew would buy into my act. I ran on the court after a questionable call and went nose to nose with him. He didn't like my tone and blew his whistle. I threw up my arms and our crowd went crazy. Richie Altenord and Cameron Jordan each grabbed one of my arms and escorted me back to the bench. Richie looked me in the eye and said, "We got your back, Coach. Let us take care of business."

It didn't change the momentum, but my players were fired up. They saw that I had their back in a tough environment, and knew we could trust each other. We lost, but learned a lot from the film going into the New Year with a record of 4-1.

Our next game was against my alma mater, Archbishop Molloy, at Long Island Lutheran. On Jan. 2nd, we watched film to correct our Baldwin mistakes and practiced to prepare for Molloy the next day. I didn't tell them much about the Stanners, but I mentioned how much I wanted to win because they were a highly ranked team. I also didn't tell them how talented and huge Molloy was this year. There would be no scouting report or pregame matchups. We were going to play the Hills West way. I asked the respected high school basketball evaluator Tom Konchalski to take a look at Kian and Richie, who were both college prospects. Tom is a wonderful person who cares deeply about high school basketball. He sat with me and longtime Molloy assistant coach Fran Leary before the game, and we shared Coach Curran stories. Coach had passed away two years earlier.

We started out down 15 points early, and I was not happy with the lack of effort from our best scorer, Kian Dalyrimple. I told the team before the game that I wanted to win to tell New York City that we still had a top-level program. We had big wins over Rice, Bishop Loughlin, and Christ the King in 2010, but this was our best chance to get it done since then. Late in the first quarter, I took out Dalyrimple and put in junior guard Matthew Asenjo, who'd gone to Molloy his freshman year. He and I had a common bond in wanting to win. Down double-digit points going into the second quarter, Matt's inspired play and our help-side defense cut the Molloy lead to two points at the half. The second half went the same way as the first. We got down early, but came storming back behind Matthew and Richie Altenord. But our comeback was a little too late. We ended up losing, and I was beyond upset. I had family and friends there to see my team play, and we didn't get it done. I select certain times to use my passionate speeches. We'd just lost our second straight game, and this was not going to continue.

Tom Konchalski came up to me afterwards and gave me one stat. He told me that Kian hadn't shot well from the field. That was the difference. I knew Kian was capable of so much more, so I was going to use my rare long postgame speech to make a point. I don't call out a person in front of their teammates, so I used my 45-minute rant to talk about everyone who played hard and gave an effort. I didn't mention his name once, and I didn't look at him at all. He got the message, and the next two weeks were spent getting him to buy into the team and play better.

In the next two weeks, I would not let Kian dribble in practice or in games. He was such a great shooter that he didn't need to dribble. After two weeks of breaking him down, he was starting to buy in. In a big game against league rival Bellport, where *Newsday*'s Bob Herzog was covering us, I told him if he dribbles, he was going to sit. He went fourteen minutes in the first half shooting without dribbling and played well. Kian dribbled the ball with two minutes left in the first half, so I took him out and told him why he was coming out. Kian was not happy. He had five points and three steals, but we were down one point at the half. Again, I really do not stand up on the sideline during games or scream at halftime. I would rather be in control and save a halftime speech for a time later in the year. This night would be no different, but Kian had a look on his face like he wanted to get back out there and crush the opposition. Cameron Jordan had that same look the year before, in the final four game against Copiague, and now I saw it in Kian. We told the guys that if we played great Hills West help-side defense, rebounded, and ran, no one could stop us.

We came out of the half with fire and intensity I hadn't seen all season. Kian got hot without dribbling and had 11 points in two minutes as the crowd started to heat up. On one play, he took a three-pointer, got slammed to the floor on the shot, and put it in. The Hills West faithful went crazy, and he hit the free throw for a rare four-point play. We pressured them again, and Kian got a steal and took two dribbles to the basket for a layup.

Bellport called timeout again to stop our momentum. I was upset Kian had dribbled twice, but my student assistant coach Jeremy Shuster grabbed me before I took him out for dribbling and said, "Coach, he's got 22 points already. The crowd is going wild and we're up 19 points. Let him go. He's on fire."

I didn't talk to them in this huddle. Sometimes, I let my assistant coaches do it and I walk away. This timeout, I went to the scorer's table to see how many points the book said he had. Coach Shuster was right to leave him in. I have learned over the years to listen and value the opinions of my assistant coaches. He finished the quarter with 27 points, and we were suddenly up 19 after being down three points early in the 3rd quarter. Kian came to the bench to a hero's welcome from his teammates. I looked at the scorer's table, and they said he had 32 points for the game. I gave him a breather and put him back in the fourth quarter. He got fouled going to the basket and hit both foul shots for his career high of 34 points. I took him out and he gave me a hug, and said with a smile, "I understand what you mean now, Coach. Catching and shooting is better than dribbling." He played amazing for the rest of the year, and I was so happy for him.

After the Molloy game in early January of 2016, I told my two assistant coaches that we weren't going to lose again for a while, and I was right. Though we lost on January 3rd, we then won 14 straight games going into the Suffolk County final four. We were given the #3 seed, and after two tough first and second-round playoff games, we went up against Northport at Stony Brook University. Northport was well coached, very methodical, and only lost one game to Baldwin HS during the regular season. Here was our approach to preparing for them. First of all, Coach Atkinson saw them play five times live, and we had film on them. I saw them play twice late in the year and trusted his assessment. We came up with a game plan, had four days to practice it, and more importantly, our guys bought in and performed beautifully. Our goal was to attack Northport and make them play our tempo. We knew we were in better shape, so we would be ready to go late in the game. The day before the game, I made a switch to the starting lineup and went small. I put Matthew Asenjo in for our usual starting center, because he looked great in practice and I had a feeling he would shoot well in a big arena. This threw off Northport. We were quicker, better defensively, and now we had four three-point shooters against the Northport zone. We played really well in the first two minutes, and Cameron Jordan got us going with his passing and defense. He had a knack for playing big in huge games, and this time was no different. Cam went to the middle of the zone and became a post passer. Cameron is a Division One wide receiver at Syracuse and has a great IQ in basketball, too. Deven

Williams and Richie Altenord did a wonderful job pressuring the ball defensively, which changed the tempo of the game for us. Kian and Matt got hot in the second half and we won easily. Matt Asenjo went for a career high 22 points, with 16 coming in the 4th quarter. We were now set up for the team that had beat us by 20 last year for the Suffolk County title: Brentwood.

We had less than 48 hours to prepare, though they had two highly recruited Division One players. I made a decision before the Northport game that we would use the same game plan for Brentwood as we did Northport. Our plan was to attack them like they had never seen from any team this year. It worked so well on Saturday that we felt it would work Monday night at Suffolk Community College. We knew their personnel, we knew their style, and I wanted to say less to them about Brentwood and more about our plan.

On Monday, it was our first day back from winter break, and the returning student body was fired up to watch us play Tuesday night. Another coach would have been overwhelmed, but I felt so prepared and confident about our mental state. We had a quick shooting practice for an hour on Monday and went home early. There have been times in my life where everything seemed to click. That night in Rockaway Beach in 1990 when Coach Graffam found me playing in a schoolyard. In 1993 at St. John's while having a great practice in front of Coach Curran was another example, and so was getting my teaching job at Hills West in 1999. These are times where you just go with the flow and life takes over. I didn't fight it, and it always seemed to work out.

We were definitely going to be the underdog, but I felt we were playing better than anyone in the county. *Newsday* had us losing, the Internet media had us losing, and my good friends Mike Quick and Rob Pavinelli at *MSG Varsity* had us losing. That was fine by me; it gave the kids the motivation to play with determination.

When I got home on Monday night for dinner at 7:30, my wife Kristen had made a wonderful turkey dinner, complete with mashed potatoes and cranberry sauce. That brought a calm over me. I can't explain the feeling, but somehow I knew we were going to win Tuesday night, and I said so at the dinner table. I could feel it, but not explain it. Call it surreal, magic, foreshadowing...call it what you will, but I felt great about the matchup. My wife knows that I get that gut feeling at times, and it usually works out for the best.

I slept great and got in the car on Tuesday morning at 6:30 a.m. like always. I turned on the ignition, and my favorite Billy Joel song came on. "Miami 2017 (The Lights Went Out on Broadway)" was an inspirational song to me, and it set the tone for me mentally in a positive way. I felt amazing driving in on Tuesday, February 23rd. I reported for school like any other Tuesday, but this day had another meaning. If we won, not only would it be a big upset, it would be our fourth Suffolk County Championship in nine years, going back to 2008. I realized the meaning of the game so early in the school day, I brought the "Core Four" to my classroom to see how they were doing emotionally. I told them how much I'd enjoyed coaching them over the last three years. They smiled with confidence, and the look in their eyes said to me they were ready to go. They were absolutely together. I couldn't tell them that I felt like we were going to win, because that would take them away from their focus.

At 5:30 p.m., as we arrived at the Suffolk Community College parking lot, the crowds were filing in despite the rain coming down in buckets. It was not a nice night to go out, but that didn't stop the fans from seeing the game of the year in Suffolk County. I had coached in several games where we played in front of thousands of people, and that didn't faze me anymore. I learned to block out the noise years ago and only focus on the game, but specifically, my team. From time to time, I will look across the way at the crowd and see my wife and kids or an old friend, but 99% of the time, I'm locked in. Before the game, I like to keep things loose, and this game was no different. My beautiful wife got to the game late with my dry cleaning, and I needed the same white collared shirt from the Northport game—our game on Sunday finished late, and I am very superstitious. A security guard from the event ran in with it from the parking lot, and I went in to get dressed while the team went back to the locker room.

In the locker room, people always think a coach will give a pregame speech like Herb Brooks before the game with the Soviet Union from the 1980 Winter Olympics. I didn't do that. Due to my clothing mishap, the kids were talking about me and not the game. It kept them loose, and I just said one thing to them. I told them something that I'd been saying all year to keep it routine. I said very calmly, "Boys, enjoy this opportunity. You've earned the right to be here, so have fun." Plenty of my former players would come back and talk to our current players. The common theme was, "Working for a living stinks, enjoy your high school basketball career and listen to Coach Mitaritonna. It's the best time of your life if you listen. So have fun with it." I have been blessed with great kids to teach and coach over the years, and the 2015-16 group was special. So I wanted them to enjoy the game.

During the warmup, the refs came over to me and said the roof was leaking in one spot, and so there would be a person wiping the floor whenever possible. It's something you can't control, so I didn't make a big deal out of it. I didn't want the kids to lose focus. The starters were announced, the national anthem was played, and the game began. Our players were ready, and I was feeling good.

The first two minutes of a game can be strange until the teams feel each other out. Kian hit a jump shot to take a 2-0 lead, but their best player, Jamel Allen, hit a traditional three-point play, and on the next possession, he stole the ball and got fouled going to the basket. I remember thinking, here we go again, like last year. That was the only time all night I felt unsure.

What was about to happen in the second quarter was outstanding and a bit shocking. Deven Williams' defense and point guard IQ were on full display. He guarded Stony Brook commit Mike Almonacy, who was the "head of the snake," and someone we had to stop. Two coaching friends of mine had given us some advice on how to defeat a very good team. "The head of the snake" reference is a metaphor. If you cut off the tail of a snake, the tail will regenerate and grow back. But the way to kill a snake is by cutting off its head. We would take away the best player on the other team by any means necessary. That's what we did to Mike Almonacy, and Deven was up for the challenge.

Deven got the ball to Kian and Cam at the right time all night. When he needed to shoot, he hit his shots. As Brentwood got into foul trouble, their defense started to break down. Up 17-12, Brentwood turned the ball over five times in a row and we went on a run. The next time I looked up at the clock during a Brentwood timeout, we were winning 28-12, and the loud and large Hills West crowd was going crazy. Andrew Bogusch, the announcer covering the game for Fios One Long Island TV, noted, "Brentwood has not been hit in the mouth like this in a long time." When you're in the moment like this in a game, you have very little control as a coach, and your players rely on training and focus.

We finished the half strong, and I practiced something all the time with my players that I felt would make an impression in this game. I gave a job to the smartest and most positive force on our bench, junior Jackson Weisbrot. When the halftime buzzer sounded, the entire team was to sprint to the locker room as a team, and I wanted to see what Brentwood would do. As time in the first half expired, Jackson led our team across the court, sprinting past the dejected Brentwood players, right in front of our cheering fans. That really helped build momentum. We went into halftime with a 38-20 lead, and we would have Richie Altenord back from foul trouble. But I knew this game was far from over.

Every time they made a run, we continued to answer. We hit 16 out of our 21 field goals attempted in the second half. Kian Dalyrimple had 20 rebounds for the game, to go along with 18 huge points. Our game plan for the last two games was attack, and we didn't stop. With 1:30 left in the game and Hills West up 16 points, Kian Dalyrimple took a charge on Jamel Allen, and he fouled out. Cameron Jordan picked up Jamel off the floor for his last varsity game. Our crowd saw our team start to hug on the court, and the sounds of screaming West fans filled the air at Suffolk Community College. We took the ball out, and Deven was fouled. He went to the line, and after he hit his first foul shot, I took out the four starters and gave a bear hug to each one as they came out. Deven completed his second free throw for a career high 28 points, and I hugged him as he came out of the game. That's when I lost it emotionally. I started to wave my hands in the air to our fans. A wave of accomplishment and excitement came over me. I never get emotionally out of control, but I was so proud of our guys. Our team was so relaxed and focused. Exactly where I wanted them mentally. It was truly a special moment for our program. They'd earned this win, and I knew how hard they'd worked to get to this point. It reminded me of my time as a walk-on at St. John's. This moment was just as special as playing in Alumni Hall in 1993. I never quit when it got tough because of the lessons taught by my parents and coaches.

We took pictures at half court, and I yelled to my team to go cele-brate with the crowd. My vision of Cameron Jordan holding the championship plaque came true, like I'd told my wife the day before. I finally noticed all of my friends from my childhood, colleagues, and members of the Hills West family, and I was able to say thank you for coming. This was a special night that I would never forget, and I took a little something from all of my coaches to win this championship. Unfortunately, we lost a week later in the Long Island Champi-onship, but I have never been more proud of a team's accomplish-ments than the 2015-16 Hills West Colts.

I gave up my position as head coach of the Hills West basketball program after the 2016-17 season to start coaching my son Brendan, and spend more time watching Jackie and Courtney's volleyball games. After seventeen seasons as the varsity coach, I will miss the relationships that are made from working with young men and teaching the game of basketball, but it was time to spend more time at home. This is a decision that I feel good about to this day. When I reflect back now, winning four Suffolk County titles and two Long

Island championships in nine seasons is something I will always appreciate, but the relationships I formed with my assistant coaches and players is what I will always cherish the most. I never coached for awards or honors, I coached to see the smiles on my players' faces after a win. Just like my father did for me.

CHAPTER TWENTY-FOUR

WHAT HAVE I LEARNED?

AS AN EDUCATOR, I always wrap up a lesson or a practice with a recap or words of wisdom. Learning is an ongoing process in life, and my wish is that this story will motivate young men and women to never give up. Goals are attainable if you put the work in, dedicate yourself, and believe you can achieve them. But I did not get to this point alone. I learned a lot from my parents and coaches. Each one helped me shape my positive outlook on life. My coaches helped me create my coaching philosophy, and how I work with young people today.

My dad showed me how to be compassionate and treat every player the same, no matter the skill level. He modeled for me how to teach without yelling, screaming, and putting kids down. There's a way to do it with dignity, and he taught me at an early age the correct way to speak.

Jack Curran showed me how to run a practice and teach the fundamentals of the game. He allowed me to be involved with the recruitment of an All-American in a high school program, the way he handled Kenny Anderson. Coach Curran modeled for me how to run a program as his student manager. All those hours in his office doing the little things paid off for me as a high school coach. After I graduated from St. John's, I went to Molloy to work as a substitute teacher and Coach Curran called me "his greatest mistake," in that he hadn't given me a chance to play. A man with over 972 career wins admitted it to me with a smile. If you knew Coach Curran, you'd know that was a compliment.

Outside of my parents, Coach Jim Graffam of Westbrook College is the most important person in my educational and coaching career. He took me out of a playground in Rockaway Beach and gave me a chance to play the game I love when no one else gave me a shot. Everything I do with my high school teams goes back to his style of play and coaching philosophy. Creating fast break opportunities on offense all comes from our defensive pressure. This isn't a new concept, but the way he taught it to me has been very successful for my teams over the years. Coach Graffam has a way of relating to players in a positive manner, which I have adopted and used with my teams. He always had my back, but he could also tell me what I was doing wrong in a non-threatening way. Coach Graffam would re-teach a concept instead of punishing us before moving on to another drill. His greatest contribution is the amazing legacy he created at Westbrook College, where he built a championship program doing it the right way.

Coach Mahoney taught me how not to change who you are as a person, no matter what the situation. He gave me the opportunity of a lifetime, and I will be forever grateful to him. Coach treated me like a scholarship player, and I will always be in his debt. Playing for St. John's has opened so many doors for me, and I love being a part of the St. John's family. A lot of coaches would not have done what he did for me, and I treat my "walk-ons" the same way: with respect and love.

I was very lucky to have mentors that I could call for advice. I asked Coach Graffam for advice after my first five years as varsity coach, and he came down from Maine to Long Island to help me at my summer basketball camp at Hills West.

I needed help with the national recruitment of Tobias Harris, and Coach Curran called me right back and gave me some great ideas. A lot of Stanners found out later in life of his generosity and love for Archbishop Molloy. Coach Curran died at the age of 82 in 2013, after 55 years of coaching baseball and basketball at Molloy. He left this Earth with a tremendous legacy of helping baseball and basketball players get to the next level. Coach Curran's wake and funeral was a testament to his dedication to high school student athletes all across the New York area.

My father Angelo was always someone I could bounce ideas off, watch video with, critique practices, or just get moral support. Unfortunately, he passed away at the age of 81 in April of 2017. That was a tough one to take, because he was always there for me unconditionally. We had three and a half days together in a hospital where he shared his last thoughts with me. Here are some notes from his last hours on Earth.

APRIL 8, 2017:

Angelo was out to lunch in New York City with his childhood friends. They were drinking beers and having a lot of laughs when my father passed out after lunch, and he was rushed to St. Luke's/Mt. Sinai Hospital, where he was diagnosed with a fatal heart condition and told he did not have long to live. I was in Philadelphia for my daughter's volleyball tournament when I got the call from my Uncle Ben. He told me it was serious, and that I should get to Manhattan as fast as I could. My wife Kristen instantly got me a ticket on AMTRAK, and I took the train into Manhattan. That was the longest two hours of my life. Not knowing the details, fearing if he were conscious. What would the doctors say? As I walked out of Penn Station in New York City, I raced to a taxi and got to the hospital in minutes. As I walked down the hall towards his room, two doctors were conferring there. They asked me who I was and asked me to sit down in an office with them. That's when my stomach dropped to the floor with fear. I spoke with the chief of neurology and a heart surgeon. Both were very respectful and broke the news to me. The heart surgeon was an Italian citizen working his residency in New York. He let me know there was nothing they could do for him. That statement did not register with me. I'd just been with him two weeks before on my birthday, and Dad had said he felt great. I couldn't help myself and started to cry.

After a few minutes, I regained my composure and let the doctors know that I should be the one to tell him. Walking from that office to his hospital room to let him know he was going to die was the toughest thing I have ever done. I tried to keep my composure, like I'd seen him handle problems his entire life. I grabbed his left hand on the side of his bed. He looked at me, relieved to see me. As I said the words, as always, Angelo was tough as nails, incredibly brave, and worried about me more than himself. His calm composure says a lot about his character. The doctors chimed in to reaffirm what I had told him. He gripped my hand, turned his head towards me, and said, "Dammit, tough break, huh, Bill?" I did not know how to respond, so I hugged him. The doctors and nurses left the room as I sobbed on his shoulder.

Later on, I told him how amazing he'd been as a father, and he responded to me, "Are you kidding me? I wish I was half the man you are, Bill." Angelo got up seven days a week for 25 straight years to work for our family without complaining. Now all he wanted was to make sure I was okay? His unselfish attitude towards life is something we can all learn from. In his weakened state, he talked about how proud he was of the job my wife and I had done in raising our kids, his grandchildren. He did not want them to come to the hospital to see him in this condition, and I agreed with his wishes.

APRIL 9TH (SUNDAY AFTERNOON):

My father said he was sorry he hadn't planned better financially; all he wanted to do was make sure I was good with money. Again, unselfish. Telling people like his brother Ben, his sister Barbara, and his sisters-in-law Arlene and Josephine was heartbreaking. But what do you do when you watch someone you immensely love and respect dying? Comfort him? Hold his hand? Tell him everything will be fine when you both know what's going to happen? It's a surreal feeling. How do you say thank you when that might not cover it? I hugged him often and cried again in front of him.

My father said, "I can't see you cry, Bill. I'm going to be okay. It's going to be all right. I had a great life."

APRIL 9TH (SUNDAY NIGHT - 7:00 P.M.):

It was starting to get dark outside. As Dad fell asleep, I put the pregame show on ESPN for the Mets game in his new hospital room. He was now receiving hospice care, and this was when it got surreal. As long as I can remember, I've had a recurring dream where I was in Manhattan overlooking the East River into Queens, looking directly at the lights coming from Shea Stadium (now Citi Field) while simultaneously watching the Mets play on TV. From his bedroom, I could look directly into Queens at the Citi Field lights, and I started to cry. I didn't know what that dream meant until now. It was my father who introduced me to the Mets and baseball in 1977, 40 years before. He always drove by the stadium for me to make me smile. Maybe it was a way of bringing us together for one last time to watch a sporting event before he passed. Or maybe he wanted me to be comfortable in this sad time. Whatever the case, Noah Syndergaard was on the mound, and the Mets won. He loved to watch Noah pitch, but he was in and out of sleep. Dad smiled at the end of the game when he saw the final score, and he forgot about his situation for a little while.

APRIL 10TH AND APRIL 11TH:

On Monday, April 10th, Dad lost his power of speech and took a turn for the worse. He passed away early Tuesday morning on my mother's birthday, April 11th. Angelo always said to remember the good times you had with someone you love. On my 45th birthday, just weeks before his passing, I drove out to eastern Long Island to see him, and we stood in his kitchen, talking like we always did when I was younger. Our talks usually included food, and on my birthday, it felt like a time warp. My father knew in his heart that I could play college basketball and believed in me without hesitation or doubt. I always felt so comfortable speaking with him, like the night I got recruited to play at Westbrook or the day I made the team at St. John's. Or sitting around a fireplace during Christmas of 2007, when he told me my story would inspire others. He called me "The Last of the Redmen" because I was the last graduating class of Redmen at St. John's in 1994. In reality, he was proud of my long journey, going from a high school student manager to a college basketball player, and now a high school coach. My father said I was "old school" in the way I taught the game of basketball, and he was so happy with the way I treated others, with respect and love. That's how I was treated at Archbishop Molloy High School, Westbrook College, and St. John's University, and that's how all players should be treated. You get more out of kids when they understand their coach is on their side. That's a lesson I will never forget.

My twelve-year-old son, Brendan, had an emotional connection with my father. It transcended genetics; the two of them had a special bond. Two months before my father passed away, he came to watch Brendan play basketball while he stayed with us in New York. In the last game my father watched Brendan play, we beat an AAU team from Brooklyn. In that game, my son scored 17 points and went 9 for 9 from the foul line. I'm convinced he played at a higher level because of my father's presence. Angelo Mitaritonna had nothing but praise for Brendan Angelo Mitaritonna after the game and bought him dinner and doughnuts. My father said the same two sentences to Brendan that he had to me, 35 years earlier.

"Brendan, I really enjoyed watching you play tonight. Did you have fun?"

My son was so excited he'd played well for his grandfather and responded with a big yes! They have very similar qualities, and after my father died, I know his spirit is still alive in my son. Brendan does something sweet for others every day that reminds me of my father. My wife and I are very lucky; there's a lot of Angelo in our son Brendan Angelo.

There's one more reason for writing this story. I want my children to know about their grandmother and grandfather, "Pee-pa," and hopefully inspire them to be good parents to their children. This story will be a way to honor my mother and father, but also teach my children about the history of our family. My parents were great role models. Parenting has made me a better teacher, and teaching has made me a better parent. I was lucky to have it both ways due to the love of my mother and father. They gave me an opportunity to succeed, and I can only hope that I continue to give that love to my wife, to my three children, and to my players in the future.

AFTERWORD

Thank you for reading my memoir.
Please go to my website www.lastoftheredmen.com
for more information on how to become a part of the "Walk-on"
community.

Feel free to view pictures and articles about
Last of the Redmen and please leave comments about my memoir if
you enjoyed the story.
Once again, thank you for reading!

ACKNOWLEDGMENTS

There were so many people who put their time and effort into the creation of *Last of the Redmen*. This is my way of saying thank you!

Thank you to my loyal friends and family who supported me while I crafted my memoir. You pushed me to finish and told me what I didn't want to hear at times. You wanted the best for me and I appreciate it!

Thank you to my editor, Max Von Zile of editingforauthors.com, for being so patient with me as I wrote my memoir.

Thank you to my freelance formatter, Jennifer Eaton of upwork.com, for guiding me through the self publishing process.

Thank you to my graphic artist and one of my favorite former students, Cristina Millan, for taking great care in creating the artwork for my story.

Thank you to my valued high school friend, Andrew Huang, for creating an inspirational promotional video for *Last of the Redmen*.

Thank you the Rosedale crew. Our friendships are coming close to 40 years. You never let me quit on my dream and you have always supported me.

Thank you to my classmates from Archbishop Molloy High

School. "Not for school, but for life" really makes sense today as we enter our 30th year as friends. Each one of you has made an important impact on my life that I can never repay.

Thank you to my teammates at Westbrook College in Portland, Maine. Our friendship has lasted over 28 years and even though we don't see each other as much as we should, we'll always have a strong bond.

Thank you to the best teachers and coaches in the state of New York! The Half Hollow Hills High School West staff inspires me to be a better teacher and your love for teaching makes it wonderful to come to work each and every day.

WE ARE...HILLS WEST!

And thank you to the Hills West basketball family. In 2000, we set out to be one of the most respected teams on Long Island and we became one of the most respected programs in New York State.

We did it TOGETHER!

LONGWOOD PUBLIC LIBRARY
800 Middle Country Road
Middle Island, NY 11953
(631) 924-6400
longwoodlibrary.org

LIBRARY HOURS

Monday-Friday	9:30 a.m. - 9:00 p.m.
Saturday	9:30 a.m. - 5:00 p.m.
Sunday (Sept-June)	1:00 p.m. - 5:00 p.m.

SA
DE
19